Carl Kalvelage
California State University, Fullerton

Morley Segal
The American University

RESEARCH GUIDE IN POLITICAL SCIENCE
2nd Edition

GENERAL LEARNING PRESS
250 James Street
Morristown, New Jersey 07960

Dedicated to our parents

Manufactured in the United States of America

Published simultaneously in Canada

Library of Congress Catalog Card Number 75-46175

ISBN 0-382-19047-5

Preface

Research Guide in Political Science is designed to keep students on target; it is intended to assist them while they are in college and after graduation. It directs students to source material that will give or restore knowledge in the field, tells how to organize and document a research paper, suggests how to use the library as a source of ideas for picking a topic, and contains advice and encouragement for those who have difficulty in formulating a hypotheses and drawing up an outline. Finally, the text contains a number of unique items to which the average undergraduate in political science will not generally be exposed (e.g., the scope and biases of the top political columnists and how to use the Freedom of Information Act).

In this second edition, we have made substantial revisions and additions both in content and in organization. The changes are based primarily on the suggestions and criticisms made by the political scientists who are now using or have used the first edition in teaching their classes. We feel that this revision is a substantial improvement over the original and that the improvement is due, in the main, to their help. We thank them.

We have added a completely new and original section on searching the literature, which we have labeled "Bridges to Information." There is also a new section on developing a research proposition and selecting the data sources, including material on quantitative methods and field research. Sources have been improved on, added to, and updated; and there are new sections on how to write a book report and political commentators in television. The section on political columnists has been updated and enlarged. A major addition is the much needed index.

We hope that students will find this research guide helpful in a variety of political science courses. We regret that there was no such guide in our own days as students.

Certain materials in the later chapters of this text are based upon corresponding sections of other research guides by General Learning Press under the consulting editorship of Carl Kalvelage. We sincerely thank the authors for their permission to use and adapt material from their texts. Also acknowledgment is made to *Editor & Publisher* magazine for permission to use their election tables.

Finally we wish to thank Kay Schmidt and the Reference Staff of The American University Library and University of Southern California Library for their time, patience, and imagination in helping us track down many hard-to-identify items and in helping us fill in difficult bibliographical details. We gratefully acknowledge the assistance given to us by John Mason Brown, *Research Resources*: *Annotated Guide to the Social Sciences*, 2 Vols., Santa Barbara, Calif.: ABC-Clio Press, 1968; *The American Reference Book Annual*, Littleton, Colo.: Libraries Unlimited, 1970; Clement E. Vose, *A Guide to Library Sources in Political Science*, Washington, D.C.: American Political Science Association, 1975; Clifton Brock, *The Literature of Political Science*, New York: R. R. Bowker, 1969.

For typing and editing efforts considerably beyond the usual, we offer our special thanks to Ruth Savoie, Mary Wason, Suzanne Baraldi, and Pamela Fazlollahi.

We, of course, accept full responsibility for all errors of fact and interpretation.

Carl Kalvelage
Morley Segal

Contents

PART ONE

1

How To Select, Develop, and Research a Topic in Political Science

The research paper is one of the basic tools of scholarship. It is the written result of careful investigation of a chosen topic and is intended to display simultaneously the student's grasp of the topic and the ability to express oneself in a scholarly fashion.

The completion of a research paper to the instructor's satisfaction indicates a *tour de force* by the student that transcends the rote of simple recall and is a badge assuring some expertise in the chosen subject. The instructor may also be assured that the student has learned where and how to search out information; how to use the library; how to take accurate notes; how to support ideas with footnotes; how to list a bibliography so that others may turn to cited sources; and, most important, how to organize his or her thoughts on a given topic.

In political science, as in every discipline, the research paper constitutes a scholar's credentials—credentials that must be earned. And to this end the following suggestions are offered as aids to choosing, researching, and writing about a topic in political science.

SELECTING A TOPIC

Selecting an initial topic can be a time-consuming and frustrating task. The problem is one of developing a focus which is both interesting and workable. Hours and hours may be spent trying to formulate an approach or researching what turns out to be an unworkable topic. A topic that may be interesting ("How to Prevent World War III") is not always manageable; that which may be manageable ("Bolivia and American Tin Quotas") might not stir the imagination.

It is important to select a topic that is not only interesting as it is originally conceived, but that will continue to hold interest throughout the difficult period of research. Choosing a topic and scanning the sources are not separate tasks; they are entwined—doing one helps in doing the other. This section, therefore, concentrates on three important steps in developing an interesting and workable topic.

A Practical Formula for Choosing a Topic

The first step in developing any formula is to define its elements; thus, one must first decide upon an initial area. To simplify this process, possible research areas have been divided into two basic groups: the *concrete* and the *abstract*. These two general areas are further divided into subgroups.

To those who are completely lost, with no hint of even a possible topic, seven of the most fertile sources in a library are offered:

Alternatives in Print
Facts on File: World News Digest
Congressional Quarterly
Foreign Affairs Bibliography
Public Affairs Information Service Index
National Party Platforms 1840-1964
Washington Information Directory

THE CONCRETE—BROWSING FOR IDEAS

There is a natural appeal to a concrete topic—that is, a topic concerned with a person, an entity or organization, an event, or a law. If one has a predisposition to investigate something, that something is likely to be one of the above concrete items. If the idea of such a topic is appealing, but it is difficult to choose which person or country would be most interesting, an hour or so of creative browsing may be rewarding. Simply thumbing through several of the resources listed on the following pages may bring several topics to mind. For convenience, these sources have been divided into four groups:

1. Persons
2. Entities (which include the whole range of human organizations from nations to neighborhood groups)
3. Events
4. Laws, programs, and policies

The most useful and general of these sources are listed in a separate section followed by the more specialized sources. In most cases the title will give a general description of the work. For a more detailed description as well as the bibliographic citation, refer to chapter 4, "Annotated Listing of Basic References."

A Person

The best general sources:
The American Political Process
Biography Index (note topical index in each volume)
Encyclopedias and Yearbooks
Congressional Quarterly Service
Dictionary of American Biography
Who Said What?
The more specialized sources:
Citizens Look at Congress
Congressional Directory

International Encyclopedia of the Social Sciences
Vital Speeches of the Day
Major Political Columnists
Facts about the Presidents
Dictionary of American Biography

An Entity or Organization

The best general sources:

United States Government Manual
Worldmark Encyclopedia of Nations
Encyclopedia of Associations
Yearbook of International Organizations
Almanac of American Politics

The more specialized sources:

Book of the States
Everyman's United Nations
Yearbook of the United Nations
Encyclopedias and yearbooks
United States in World Affairs
Comparative International Almanac
Municipal Yearbook
The Role of Political Parties in Congress

Events

The best general sources:

Congressional Quarterly Service
Congress and the Nation
News Dictionary
An Encyclopedia of World History
Facts on File: World News Digest

The more specialized sources:

America Votes
New York Times Index
World Almanac and Book of Facts
Foreign Affairs Bibliography
The Annual Register of World Events
Guide to the Diplomatic History of the United States
The Vietnam Conflict

Laws, Policies, and Programs
    The best general sources:
        Congressional Quarterly Service
        Congressional Information Service Index
        Subject Guide to Major Government Publications
        National Party Platforms 1840-1964
        Yearbook of the United Nations
        Washington Lobby
    The more specialized sources:
        Everyman's United Nations
        *The Constitution of the United States of America:
            Analysis and Interpretation*
        Gallup Opinion Index
        Municipal Yearbook
        Poverty in the United States During the Sixties
        Public Affairs Information Service Index
        United States Government Manual
        New York Times Guide for Federal Aid
        Vital Speeches of the Day
        Weekly Compilation of Presidential Documents
        Universal Reference System

THE ABSTRACT–BROWSING FOR IDEAS

Classifying ideas and abstractions has been the pursuit of philosophers for centuries. Since the purpose of this book is to use ideas in a practical fashion to help focus and organize proposed papers, a very simple three-fold classification will be adopted for abstract topics.

1. *Values*: ideas and concepts implying desirability
2. *Problems*: ideas and concepts implying undesirability
3. *Process*: ideas and concepts that imply neither desirability nor undesirability

To be more explicit, "value" refers to any concept or idea that describes an interest, pleasure, moral obligation, desire, want, need, etc. It may refer to a measurable activity, like equal opportunity in employment, or to an intangible, such as "support for the regime."

"Problem," the second organizational classification, may also refer to a measurable activity or a feeling, but it is generally regarded as an undesirable, such as a feeling of political alienation, or apathy.

"Process" has no connotation of desirability or undesirability but simply refers to any observable or definable pattern in activities of people and groups. "Political process" refers to the pattern that emerges from the behavior of people and groups as they strive for and use political power.

Many ideas or concepts can be placed in two or even all three of these categories—depending upon the intent of the holder. President Ford's pardon of Richard Nixon, for instance, can be treated as a neutral process, a grave problem, or a boon to the republic. How one regards these ideas depends upon one's own attitudes. The categories of value, problem, and process simply help in identifying one's own feelings toward these ideas in order to use them in organizing a paper.

All three abstract concept classifications have one thing in common: as ideas, they cannot be seen, heard, or felt. Often they are not even recognized by those involved but are abstractions, imposed upon them by an outside observer. (For example, look at the process of a group of grade-school children saluting the flag. Neither these children nor their teacher may realize that they are involved in the "process of political socialization," but they would be observed as such by many political scientists.)

Whatever one's preference for political description, these three categories of abstract ideas will be invaluable for organizing thoughts and ideas into a paper. Since most source books deal with ideas and concepts applicable to all three categories, they have been listed together. If a research source is especially relevant to one category, this has been indicated in parentheses.

Abstractions: Values, Problems, and Process
    The best general sources:
        A Cross Polity Survey
        Glossary of Ideas
        The Syntopicon Volumes
        Universal Reference System
        Masterpieces of World Philosophy in Summary Form
        The New Language of Politics
        All About Politics
        Editorial Research Reports
        Public Affairs Information Service Index (especially for
            problems)
        *ABS Guide to Recent Publications in the Social and
            Behavioral Sciences* (process)
        International Encyclopedia of Social Sciences
        Social Sciences Index
        Vital Speeches of the Day
        *Doctoral Dissertations in Political Science in Universities
            in the United States*
    The more specialized sources:
        Congressional Digest
        *The Constitution of the United States of America:
            Analysis and Interpretation*
        Essay and General Literature Index
        Weekly Compilation of Presidential Documents
        Index to Legal Periodicals
        Foreign Affairs Bibliography
        National Party Platforms 1840-1964 (problems)
        Readers' Guide to Periodical Literature
        Congressional Quarterly Service
        Congress and the Nation
        Subject Guide to Major Government Publications
        Working on the System

    As one begins to explore the material, it is usually
discovered that far more has been written on the chosen topic
than expected. The traditional advice is to "narrow" the topic,

but this is only a partial answer, for "narrowing" in the traditional way can squeeze the life out of an interesting topic. The next section demonstrates how to narrow a topic and still keep it interesting.

DEVELOPING A TOPIC

What is usually called "narrowing down" refers to the process of reducing a topic in terms of either time or space. Instead of writing about Robert Kennedy's entire life, the topic may be reduced to the months he spent working for Senator Joseph McCarthy. Instead of writing about Mexican politics, a paper on politics in Sonora province might be developed. The project now appears to become manageable, but it may not be, actually, because one still may find that there is far more written about politics in Sonora province or about this period in Robert Kennedy's life than can be dealt with in a term paper. When a topic is finally narrowed down, it often is so narrow that it becomes a task even to state the title. On the other hand, if it is decided not to narrow the topic down, coverage may be so superficial that originality is sacrificed.

Another choice is available in reducing a topic: the development of a sharper focus in terms of interesting and worthwhile questions that might be answered about the chosen topic, questions that will help define what is relevant and what is not for research.

The problem is now to identify these questions. One method is to combine the categories of the abstract and concrete; for example, the topic of Ralph Nader (concrete) and the idea of "Free Enterprise" (an abstract value). There are a great many possible combinations of these categories. To help in identifying some of the possibilities for a selected topic, three charts have been constructed:

1. Combining the concrete and the abstract
2. Combining one abstraction with another
3. Combining two concrete objects

Tables 1, 2, and 3 develop these possibilities further.

TABLE 1 / Combining the Concrete and the Abstract

	Process	Problem	Value
Person	Sen. Edmund Muskie and the new congressional budget process	Richard Nixon and the alienation of American youth	Will Rogers and the development of American political satire
Event	The election of 1928 and the growth of the New Deal coalition	The Treaty of Versailles and the rise of Adolph Hitler	The War of 1812 and the tradition of political dissent
Entity	The Sierra Club and the mobilization of public opinion on conservation	The Irish Republican Army (IRA) and violence in Northern Ireland	The Anti-Federalists and the development of the idea of citizen participation in administration
Law or Policy	Aid to Latin America and the congressional appropriation process	The First Amendment and the problem of obscenity in the mail	Revenue sharing and the decentralization of authority from national to local governments

TABLE 2 / Combining Two Abstractions as a Focus

	Process	Problem	Value
Process	The conflict between internal congressional and constituent pressures upon Congresswoman Shirley Chisholm	The election of federal judges and the problem of conflict of interest	The development of political attitudes in the comic strip "Peanuts"
Problem	Presidential press relations: the problems of Richard Nixon	Organized crime, wiretapping, and the right of privacy	Rational choice in presidential elections and the threat of television image-making
Value	The impact of capital punishment on prison discipline	The publication of the Pentagon Papers and the protection of government secrecy	Speed vs. thoroughness: drug testing problems of the FDA

TABLE 3 / Combining Two Concrete Objects of Study on the Basis of an Abstraction

	Person	Event	Entity	Law or Policy
Person	Gary Hart and John Glenn as freshmen senators: a comparison	George McGovern and the Democratic Convention of 1972	George Wallace and his impact on organized labor	U Thant and the development of UN police action
Event	Mayor Richard Daley and the election of John F. Kennedy in 1960	A comparison of two campaigns: Henry Wallace, 1948; George Wallace, 1968	The AMA and the passage of Medicare	The energy crisis and agricultural price supports
Entity	Henry Kissinger and the reorganization of the Department of State	The American Legion and the Vietnam War	Kenya and Tanzania: a comparison of electoral processes	The Office of Passports and Cuba
Law or Policy	Secretary of Defense Schlesinger and the use of nuclear weapons	School busing and the election of the President in 1972	The Clean Air Act and General Motors	Two approaches to saving energy: the independent Federal Energy Administration and the Office of Energy Conservation in the Department of the Interior

SEARCHING THE LITERATURE AND
DEVELOPING A PROPOSITION

In all likelihood, more is written about your topic than you will be able to use in a single research paper. Your goal is to identify the relevant and available material, taking care to avoid being overburdened with

1. More material than you can read or use
2. Material that is outdated, not directly related to your topic, or beyond the scope of your understanding
3. The expenditure of large amounts of time searching for material not available in your library

In the latter regard, we have identified the following basic bridges to information:

1. Card catalog
2. Bibliographies
3. Indexes
4. Abstracts and digests

Some of these bridges are more basic than others—and are therefore listed first. Unless your topic is highly specialized, these will be your most helpful sources.

Before you begin your search you should narrow your topic as much as possible and also think about the possible ways your topic might be listed. For example, if you were concerned with the role of the CIA (Central Intelligence Agency) in Watergate, the problem would be simple. You could look up the CIA or Watergate (most likely a subhead under United States Government and Politics—1960-). If, however, you were re-searching something a bit more abstract, such as how Watergate influenced the attitudes of young people about government in 1974, you would have to look under more general headings such as Public Opinion—U.S. or U.S.—Social Life and Customs. (For more about using the card catalog, see pages 16-18.)

Creative thought does not always take place in orderly steps. It would be nice if one could neatly define a research project then search the library for sources. More likely is the process in which you begin to define your project, search the literature, and as you see what is available, refine your topic. For this reason we are presenting the next step in topic development, *defining a proposition,* as something to consider *while* you are searching the literature. After a topic is defined, the next step is to define a proposition or hypothesis. Many students falter at this step; perhaps the term *hypothesis* has a threatening and ponderous ring to it, but it is really a very simple matter.

A proposition or hypothesis is a statement that your paper can either prove or disprove. For example, "The Irish Republican Army (IRA) and violence in Northern Ireland" could yield a number of provable or disprovable statements, such as:

1. Increases in British troop strength in Northern Ireland are usually followed by IRA violence. (You could just as easily have used decreases in troop strength.)
2. Philosophical justification for IRA violence can be found in the works of William Butler Yeats.
3. Speeches in the British Parliament during the first six months of 1972 were more critical of the IRA than were those during the last six months.
4. The Labor Party in Great Britain has in the last six years been more sympathetic in its official statements to Catholics in Northern Ireland than to Protestants there.

All the above are propositions because they are stated in such a way that they can be proven or disproven.

The following is not a testable proposition: oppression by the British has caused the use of violence in Northern Ireland. This proposition might be true, but it would be very hard to prove in a standard research paper. The misleading advantage of having such a proposition is that it serves as a "fishing license" for you to research anything you want. This advantage is more than offset by the disadvantage, which is that neither you nor your reader will ever really be sure you have accomplished your task, for the task has not been defined. Unless you simply enjoy the process of endless research, we suggest that you develop testable propositions.

As you complete your basic literature search, jot down testable propositions as they occur to you. After you discover what is available, you can consider which proposition you actually wish to test.

Bridges to Information

THE CARD CATALOG—YOUR FIRST STEP

The card catalog is your first and primary bridge to information. It is especially useful because, unlike other guides, nothing will be listed there that your library does not have. Usually, every book in the library will be listed on at least three cards:

1. Title card
2. Author card
3. Subject card (There may be several of these.)

Assuming that you do not know what specific book you are looking for, it is the subject card that will be of most help to you. The problem is to identify the subject. If it is a concrete subject, such as John F. Kennedy, you have no problem. Books about Kennedy will be identified by a typed subject heading over the title. (See top of following page.)

If, however, your topic is a bit more abstract—"Kennedy and Business," for example—you will have to take one figurative step back and decide what general process or subject you are dealing with and how this subject might be labeled in the card catalog. In this instance, it is "Industry and the State—U.S." One aid in figuring out these categories is the cross references at the bottom of the card in the following example.

Another problem is that a particular political process can be identified in several ways. For example, if you

HD
3616   KENNEDY, JOHN FITZGERALD, PRES. U.S., 1917-
.U47R69   1963
          Rowen, Hobart.
          The free enterprisers: Kennedy, Johnson, and the busi-
          ness establishment. New York, Putnam [1964]

          319 p.   22 cm.

          Bibliographical references included in "Notes" (p. 298-310)

          1. Industry and state—U. S. 2. Kennedy, John Fitzgerald,
          Pres. U. S., 1917-1963. 3. Johnson, Lyndon Baines, Pres. U. S.,
          1908- I. Title.

          HD3616.U47R69   338.973   64–23089

          Library of Congress   [64f14]

look up campaign finance, you will find the following
scholarly book:

                    CAMPAIGN FUNDS
          JK
          1991
          .A714   **Alexander, Herbert E**
                    Political financing. Minneapolis,
                    Burgess [1972]
                    60 p. (Critical issues in political
                    science)

                    Bibliography: p. 59-60.

                    1. Elections-U.S.-Campaign funds. 2.
          Campaign funds. I. Title.

If, however, you want to know how presidential campaigns
are financed, you will have to look under the general
heading "Elections-U.S.-Campaign Funds," where you will
find the following:

ELECTIONS – U.S. – CAMPAIGN FUNDS

JK
1991
.D85   Dunn, Delmer D
                    Financing presidential campaigns. Wash-
              ington, D.C., The Brookings Institution
              ₍1972₎
                    xiii, 168 p. (Studies in presidential
              selection)

              Bibliographical footnotes.

                    1. Elections – U.S. – Campaign funds. 2. Pres-
              dents-U.S.-Election. I. Title. II. Series.

It is impossible to guess all the subject listings that can be found in the card catalog; however, the following five tactics can help:

1. Ask yourself, "What is the general subject or process, and where is it taking place?" Example: Elections–U.S.
2. Find a card for one book even vaguely related to the subject and check the cross listings on the bottom of the card.
3. Consult the "See" and "See also" cards in the subject catalog.
4. Look at *Subject Headings Used in the Dictionary Catalogs of the Library of Congress* (Washington, D.C.: Library of Congress, 1966). This is a master list of subject headings. Look up what *you* are calling your subject, and the list will refer you to the *catalog* heading.
5. Ask the librarian.

SHELF BROWSING–YOUR SECOND STEP

All libraries use one of the two subject classification systems described below. Once you locate the *several* areas where books on your subject are shelved, you can simply browse. Remember, however, to double-check the card catalog to identify the various subject headings.

The following explanation of library classification systems will help you locate the proper section.

Dewey Decimal Classification

Melvil Dewey worked out this approach in the latter part of the nineteenth century. The Dewey decimal classification system divides all knowledge, as represented by books and other materials that are acquired by libraries, into nine main classes, which are numbered by the digits 1 to 9. Material too general to belong to any one of these classes, such as newspapers and encyclopedias, falls into a tenth class, numbered 0, which precedes the others. The classes are written as hundreds; thus, 000 is general works, 100 is philosophy, 200 is religion, 300 is social sciences, and so on. Each division is again divided into nine sections preceded by a general section; thus, 300 is the social sciences in general, while 321 is forms of state, 322 the state and religion, 323 the relationship between states and individuals or groups, etc. Further division to bring together like materials is accomplished by the addition of digits following a decimal point. Usually, most numbers do not exceed six digits in length, i.e., three to the right of the decimal point; however, there are cases of numbers extending to nine or more digits.

The basic classification system ranges from 000 to 999:

000–099	General works
100–199	Philosophy
200–299	Religion
300–399	Social sciences
400–499	Language
500–599	Pure sciences
600–699	Technology
700–799	Arts
800–899	Literature
900–999	History

The broad category of most relevance to political scientists is 300-399, the social sciences.

300–309	The social sciences, general
310–319	Statistics
320–329	Political science
330–339	Economics
340–349	Law
350–359	Public administration
360–369	Social welfare
370–379	Education
380–389	Public services and utilities
390–399	Customs and folklore

The specific category of most relevance to this study is that of "political science" (320-329), which is broken down into ten subclasses, each of which may be further subdivided by the use of decimals. For example, the subclass 326, "slavery," then becomes 326.1, "slave trade"; 326.2, "coolies and contract slaves"; 326.3, "serfs and serfdom"; etc.

320	Political science, general
321	Forms of states
322	State and church
323	State and individual
324	Suffrage and elections
325	Migration and colonization
326	Slavery
327	Foreign relations
328	Legislation
329	Political parties

For the complete list of subclassifications, see the *Dewey Decimal Classification and Relative Index*, 18th ed., 2 vols. (New York: Forest Press, of Lake Placid Club Education Foundation, 1970).

Library of Congress Classification

The Library of Congress classification system was adopted in 1900, three years after the Library of Congress moved from the Capitol to its new building. The library changed systems in order to have a more systematic and functional arrangement of its collection.

This system divides the fields of knowledge into twenty groups by assigning a letter to each and combining arabic numerals and additional letters to separate the main groups into classes and subclasses in a way similar to that used in the Dewey decimal system. All books are divided into the following basic groups:

A	General works	M	Music
B	Philosophy and religion	N	Fine arts
C	History and auxiliary sciences	P	Language and literature
		Q	Science
D	Foreign history and topography	R	Medicine
		S	Agriculture
E-F	American history	T	Technology
G	Geography and anthropology	U	Military science
H	Social science	V	Naval science
J	Political science	Z	Bibliography and library science
K	Law		
L	Education		

For political scientists, class J (political science) is the most relevant. Within each class, subdivisions are denoted by a second letter. Thus for political science, we have the following subclasses:

J	Official documents
JA	General works
JC	Political theory
JF	Constitutional history and administration
JK	United States
JL	British America, Latin America
JN	Europe
JQ	Asia, Africa, Australia, Pacific Islands
JS	Local government
JV	Colonies and colonization
JX	International law and international relations

Each subclass makes up several smaller regional, historical, or functional subdivisions. For the complete list of subclassifications see *Classification: Class J, Political Science,* 2nd ed. (Washington, D.C.: Government Printing Office, 1924; reprinted in 1966).

ENCYCLOPEDIAS

Most people instinctively turn to a general reference encyclopedia as their first source of reference, as this is the most convenient source of quick information in the library. A good encyclopedia contains not only a great deal of important substantive information but also useful bibliographies, cross references, and other guides to help in conducting further research. Encyclopedias, however, vary in at least three important ways:

1. Quality. Many encyclopedias are authoritative and scholarly, but some are neither. Only those encyclopedias generally accepted as reliable by teachers, librarians, and scholars are listed on pages 99-102.
2. Depth. Some encyclopedias are designed for grade school and high school use, some for popular adult use, and others for scholarly use at the college level. Included here are only those suitable for research at the college level; excluded are many excellent works such as the *World Book,* which is designed for elementary, high school, and general adult use.
3. Scope. While the term *encyclopedia* denotes an all-inclusive approach, even encyclopedias specialize. Under the proper title, strong points of each set are indicated. (See the section on Encyclopedia Bibliography, p. 99.)

There are over twenty-five full length encyclopedias published in the United States. In this guide we have included only those adult general encyclopedias which have received a rating of "top quality, very highly recommended" in the definitive reference work, *General*

Encyclopedias in Print 1971-72, compiled by S. Padraig Walsh. New York: R. R. Bowker, 1971.

Bibliographies

If card catalogs could include subject listings for every important aspect of a book, booklet, magazine article, or other source, there would be no need for bibliographies. The fact is, however, that the subject listing is so broad that it is rare to find one precisely fitting your topic. Furthermore, there are probably important sources, such as periodicals, that are not listed in the catalog. In such cases, the most helpful bridge is a bibliography, that is, a list of publications on a given subject. If you know the subject heading, bibliographies will be listed in the card catalog under that heading. If you do not, then you must turn to the next best source for bibliographies: *Bibliographic Index* (p. 77), *Universal Reference System* (p. 78), and more specialized bibliographies (p. 78).

In addition, there are several general indexing and bibliographic guides. These cover a broad range of subjects but can provide bibliographies in a variety of areas within a particular field. Their strength—and their weakness—lies in their scope. You can almost always locate a source for your topic in these books, but you may have to look in more than one place. Nevertheless, you should learn how to use each and to realize the various ways in which your topic might be categorized. (See General Bibliographies, p. 76.)

In addition to the general bibliographies, there are a number of special subject area bibliographies. There are three basic types of these bibliographies, each appropriate for a different need.

1. Book length bibliographies—exhaustive lists usually containing virtually everything published on a given topic. They can give you a good feel for the depth and breadth of a particular subject area. The better of these large bibliographies are broken down into subcategories,

which help reduce their massiveness. The Deutsch and Merritt bibliography on *Nationalism and National Development* listed on page 82 is a good example of such a reference work.

2. Bibliographic essays. These describe a field, its scope, and the issues within it—and at the same time place citations in various categories. A good example of this is *The Role of Political Parties in Congress,* cited on page 80. Many bibliographic essays appear as journal articles. See, for instance, Clement E. Vose, "Political Dictionaries: A Bibliographic Essay," *American Political Science Review* 68 (December 1974), which we cite later. The best way to find these essays is through the periodical indexes described on pages 105-110.

3. Bibliographies in books and articles. These can be located through the *Bibliographic Index* and the various periodical indexes.

PERIODICAL INDEXES

If your paper depends solely on books and ignores periodicals, it is likely to lack important *current* material. Periodical citations are also considered by many instructors as a sign that a student has carried out at least a minimum of original research. Most useful of the indexes are the *Public Affairs Information Service* (for popular and documentary material, p. 105) and the *Social Sciences Index* (for academic material, p. 105). We also might mention again the *Universal Reference System* (p. 78). Should you wish to probe more deeply into your topic, these specialized indexes will be helpful: magazine indexes (p. 106), newspaper indexes (p. 106), and other special purpose indexes (p. 107).

ABSTRACTS AND DIGESTS

Abstracts are indexes with concise summaries of the main points of the articles listed. They give a glimpse of the content of an article (to help you decide whether or not to track it down) and allow you to rapidly survey a field without actually searching out the original articles. Most abstracts and digests are by necessity specialized. The most generally useful is *The American Political Process* (p. 74). Other useful abstracts are listed on pages 74-76.

LOCATING THE DATA TO TEST A PROPOSITION

Once you have searched the literature and developed a testable proposition, the next step is to decide how to test it. Rather than pick a particular research method or technique, first ask: "What information could test this proposition and where is it located?" The answer to this question will then help you select from the many research methods and techniques available in modern political science.

To illustrate this process, we will discuss a proposition related to the topic "Federal Revenue Sharing and the Value of Decentralization of Authority from National to Local Governments."

Proposition: The majority of new revenue from the revenue sharing program has been spent for additional hardware such as a new fire engine rather than for social programs such as welfare.

Table 4 shows how this proposition can be tested by means of a variety of techniques using the sources in this guide.

Data to test this or any other proposition you might devise can be divided into two broad categories: documentary and live.

Documentary Data

Documentary data include the variety of written material available in the library and elsewhere. Documentary data can be both primary and secondary. Primary data represent an initial response to an inquiry. How many people in New York voted for George McGovern in 1972? What is the birth rate in India? Data are secondary if they constitute an analysis refinement or an account of primary data—such as is found in Carl Gershman

TABLE 4 / Proposition: The majority of new revenue from the revenue sharing program has been spent for additional hardware such as a new fire engine rather than for social programs such as welfare.

Location of Data to Test Proposition	Possible Technique	Some Relevant Library Data Sources and Guides to Information in This Guide
Documentary Data: *Primary*	Contextual and statistical analysis	
Reports from the Office of Revenue Sharing		*Monthly Catalogue of U.S. Government Publications* *Social Indicators* *American Statistics Index* *Setting National Priorities*
Reports from interest groups and individuals		*What They Said In* *The Washington Lobby* *National Trade and Professional Assoc. National Journal*
Congressional debate, votes, and hearings		*Congressional Record* *Congressional Quarterly Weekly Report* *Congressional Roll Call* *Congressional Information Service Index*
Reports from state and local governments		*Book of the States* *Municipal Yearbook* *Congressional District Data Book* *County and City Data Book* *Index to Current Urban Documents*
Documentary Data: *Secondary*		
Popular and academic accounts		*Metropolitan Annual* *Public Affairs Information Service* *Urban Affairs Bibliography*

TABLE 4 (continued)

Location of Data to Test Proposition	Possible Technique	Some Relevant Library Data Sources and Guides to Information in This Guide
Media coverage	Content analysis	
Live Data: Interviews		
In the minds of relevant officials at national, state, and local levels	Elite interviewing	
In the minds of citizens (if issue has achieved public visibility)	Survey research	Gallup Poll Harris Poll Regional polls
Can use direct questions if not questions concerning how they perceive levels of local service, i.e., fire service vs. welfare		
Live Data: Observation		
Behavior in public meetings		*Inventory of Human Behavior* (a secondary source of ideas)*
Behavior at points of local service delivery		

· ·

*Each entry in column 3 has a detailed description and bibliographic citation in Chapter 4, "Annotated Listing of Basic References."

and Steven Kelman, "Labor's Stand on McGovern, Two Views," *New Leader,* September 4, 1972. The preceding would also be considered a primary source if it included a new statement by a labor leader on George McGovern's 1972 candidacy.

The term *documentary data* suggests the use of a technique we describe as the politics of documentation. This simply means searching a document for the context in which the data are presented. These techniques are explained in an old, but still useful, source: E. E. Schattscheider, Victor Jones, and Stephen K. Bailey, *A Guide to the Study of Public Affairs* (New York: William Sloane, 1951). This guide points out precisely what to look for when one reads a budget or a judicial decision, attempts to study a pressure group, or examines a number of other sources. It points out that documentary evidence may thus be taken at two levels: what is said and the context in which it is stated.

In addition to the politics of documentation approach, you may utilize the behavioral techniques of content analysis. Content analysis involves counting the frequency or manner in which a particular topic is suggested. For example, using our illustration of revenue sharing, one could read the *Congressional Record* on the subject and analyze the number and type of references to "home rule." For additional material on content analysis, see Ole Holsti, *Content Analysis* (Reading, Mass.: Addison Wesley, 1969). These techniques are appropriate to a wide variety of written material—of which government documents are but one prime example.

GOVERNMENT DOCUMENTS

Finding government documents is likely to be a multistep process. They are usually listed by the issuing agency, so your first step is to find which agency (or, more likely, agencies) is connected to the subject that you are investigating. The basic guide to federal agencies is the *United States Government Manual* (p. 130). Another guide, although a bit outdated (1968), is *Subject Guide to Major*

Government Publications (p. 102), which aims at such current problems as "energy" and "environment."

The next step is to find the document itself. The basic index for government publications is the *Monthly Catalog of U.S. Government Publications* (p. 144). Each issue now has author, title, and subject indexes. The government also issues many periodicals, and each February the monthly catalog lists these in an appendix. For your further guidance, there is an annual cumulative index included in the December issue of the monthly catalog. The years 1941 to 1950 are covered in *A Decennial Cumulative Index 1941-1950*; the years 1951 through 1960 are covered in *A Decennial Cumulative Index 1951-1960*.

The most useful index to current congressional publications is *Congressional Information Service Index to Publications of the U.S. Congress* (p. 102).

The most important source *about* government publications is the now classic *Government Publications and Their Use* (p. 102). The student also should look over the section in this text on Specialized Guides (p. 103, 157).

Quantitative Data

Another type of primary documentation is quantitative data. Again, just as important as the data themselves is an understanding of their context and possible bias. Two good sources to aid your understanding of this context are Darrell Huff, *How to Lie with Statistics* (New York: Norton, 1954) and John Phillips, *Statistical Thinking: A Structural Approach* (San Francisco: Freemen, 1973). See also Chapter 7.

The manipulation and interpretation of quantitative data have been a prime focus in political science over the past two decades. Quantitative methodology involves the logic of scientific inquiry as well as collecting, comparing, manipulating, and analyzing data.

The quantitative approach is so complex that many political science departments now have courses in such methods at the undergraduate level. Because only a few of the many books on quantitative methodology are understandable by most students who have not had such a class, we recommend reading W. Phillips Shively, *The Craft of Political Research: A Primer* (Englewood Cliffs, N.J.: Prentice-Hall, 1974).

USING QUANTITATIVE TECHNIQUES
WITH LIBRARY MATERIALS

The library is a rich source of quantitative data, much of which can be used without elaborate statistical training. Unless you have a particular reason to experience the time-consuming process of collecting data, we suggest that you explore your library sources first. Bridges to these sources can be found on pages 84-85. Also, this text contains a special section on statistics (pp. 85-95).

Secondary Documentary Data

The easiest way to define secondary documentary data is to identify primary data and then say that secondary data is everything that is left: comments, reviews, interpretations, essays, etc. The bulk of secondary data can be found in the section on Special Subjects.

Two forms of secondary data, however, deserve special attention while you are still formulating your project: doctoral dissertations (which often contain primary data as well) and book reviews.

DISSERTATIONS

Only the students writing advanced and specialized papers will want to utilize doctoral dissertations as sources. Dissertations do, however, have some unique qualities. They are thorough, usually original, include a chapter on the research methods used, and contain an exhaustive bibliography. Often, the major points of a dissertation may be found in an abstract, so the entire manuscript need seldom be obtained. Moreover, just going down a list of dissertation titles can help one choose a topic and perhaps suggest an original approach to that topic.

The following are the main sources of dissertations: *Dissertation Abstracts* (p. 99) and *Doctoral Dissertations in Political Science in Universities in the United States* (p. 99).

Book Reviews

Book reviews are an especially important secondary source and so have a legitimate place in research work for term papers. But they must always be viewed as a supplement to, not a substitute for, reading the original. Read a book review before reading the book and you will find it easier to pick out the main points; read the review after reading the book and you have a laboratory check on the difference between your thinking and the reviewer's. But do not hesitate to cite the opinions of reviewers when dealing with a book upon which your paper is relying. (See Book Reports, p. 170. Note that the authors have devoted a section of this book to explaining the mechanics of writing a book report or review.)

Live Data

Although a great deal of primary data is available in the library, perhaps you will want to have the experience of collecting data firsthand. Most methodological works point out the relatively higher time cost of gathering information first-hand. Thus, the question one must ask before deciding to generate his own data is: Are the available sources of data inadequate to test this proposition?

If so, one can turn to the two basic sources of live data: interviewing and observation.

INTERVIEWING

There are two types of interviewing: elite interviewing and survey research. In elite interviewing, one questions a relatively small number of people who have a relatively large amount of information on a particular subject, e.g., a legislator, mayor, etc. Elites almost by definition are very busy people and are in a sense a perishable data source. If you are unprepared to ask intelligent questions, or if you ask questions that are easily answerable from public records, you might well find the interview abruptly cut short. Elite interviewing is an art involving a personal transaction between you and the interviewee. The best discussion of this sophisticated art is in Lewis Anthony Dexter, *Elite and Specialized Interviewing: Handbooks for Research in Political Behavior* (Evanston, Ill.: Northwestern University Press, 1970).

Some much more basic rules and techniques (mostly don'ts) are paraphrased from the American University Washington Semester Program instructions to undergraduate interviewers:

1. Try to make an appointment. Do not just "drop in" on a busy official unless he has invited you to do so, or unless you have been unable to get his office to give you an appointment.
2. Be prompt for appointments. Leave a sufficient safety margin in your travel time to the appointment to cover accidental delays and getting lost.
3. While waiting to be shown in, verify the spelling of the name and title of the official you are going to interview, and the pronunciation of his name, if in doubt. Write these things down for your bibliography and other later uses. Mark down the date of the interview.
4. Ask the secretary, also, for printed materials that might be available.

5. Begin the interview by telling who you are, why you are doing the project, and what it is about.

6. Have several specific questions prepared, covering your purpose for being there. These should be ones which fill necessary gaps remaining in your information after you have done all the reading for the project. These questions may then lead to others.

7. Take notes only with permission, and even then, only if you are sure that doing so will not destroy the usefulness of the interview. Sometimes it is better to wait until the interview is over to take down what was said.

8. Do not quote one official to another!

9. Thank the person interviewed and leave just as soon as you feel that you have the information you need, unless he is clearly not busy and is willing to talk further. Don't overstay your welcome.

10. Write a note of thanks to the person interviewed within a week. This should be regarded as a strict obligation. No single act does more for the benefit of future students seeking similar interviews.

Remember that you are carrying the reputation of your college on your shoulders when interviewing. If you leave behind you a trail of irritation, or if you present yourself ill-prepared, or if you fail to show decent courtesy and gratitude, you will make life that much harder for other students who may come later to interview the same people.

As a final note about interviewing, bear in mind that you are doing serious research. The number of interviews is far less important than the quality of the information gained. Seek out the knowledgeable, not the garrulous, and ask each interviewee for suggestions for future interviews.

Survey research, on the other hand, involves interviewing a representative sample of, for example, citizens or government workers on a matter in which they are not experts and might not even be interested. Their lack of knowledge or interest is itself data, and you will have to find a systematic way to record their nonresponse. Survey research thus involves selecting a representative sample from a larger population—and making this selection without biasing the results can be difficult.

The relatively large numbers of respondents and the possible low level of knowledge or interest means that a carefully constructed questionnaire with coded answers must also be devised. If elite interviewing as described by Dexter is an art, then survey research must resemble a science. One exposition of the intricacies of this form of scientific endeavor is Charles Backstrom and Gerald Hursh, *Survey Research* (Evanston, Ill.: Northwestern University Press, 1963).

OBSERVATION

There are certain kinds of information that are available only through firsthand observation. For example, only by actually observing city council meetings could one capture the full debate, because in many cities there is only the most minimal public record or media coverage. Likewise, only by observing a local public health center could one find out how long individuals have to wait before they are treated. A significant variation of observation is experimentation—where the researchers themselves provide the stimuli for an observation. An example would be asking councilmen a pointed question at a public meeting. Such experimentation must be done more than once on a systematic basis in order to develop comparable data. There is no single source on observation and experimentation. The following is the best overall source:

Eugene Webb, et al, *Unobtrusive Measures: Non-Reactive Research in the Social Sciences* (Chicago: Rand McNally, 1966).

SUMMARY

In the preceding pages we have described some basic steps to help focus your research efforts:

1. Selecting a topic
2. Selecting a testable proposition
3. Identifying the information that will help you test your proposition

Table 4, pages 26-27, illustrates these steps for a proposition regarding revenue sharing. This table illustrates the almost infinite possibilities by which one can investigate a problem using primary data, most of which are available in the library. At least four types of information leading to four different research strategies are shown. It is likely that any one of these approaches would be satisfactory for a research paper.

TAKING NOTES

Now the material gathered by the student must be read and from it all pertinent information extracted. The resultant research notes should be transcribed clearly and concisely. The best and easiest way is to use 4 X 6 or 5 X 8 index cards, lined or unlined, on which to note the pertinent data. On these the name of the author, title of the book, the edition, the publisher's name, place of publication, date of publication, and volume number are also written. It goes without saying, of course, that the page or pages where the material was found should be recorded, too.

If the material is contained in a journal, the necessary data include the author, title of the article, name of the journal, volume number, date of publication, and the page numbers of the article. In either case, the library classification number should be added so that if the material needs to be rechecked, it can be easily located. A separate card, of course, should be used for each source and, later on, each idea or quotation. In the latter case, note the source in an abbreviated form with the appropriate page references.

When an author is paraphrased, care should be taken to assure that his intent is not distorted; when quoting, the quote must be exact. Notes generally should be as brief as is practical, but should they run to length, the student will serve himself well to number each card used in sequence.

2

Putting It All Together

The original sources have now been read and gleaned of all material that will give some form to the preliminary skeletal outline. It is all there on the index cards, waiting to be shaped by the students. They should read the notes carefully, gaining in this manner a comprehensive overview of the material; they should become aware of supporting and contradicting material, and then—using the rough draft as a guide—begin mentally building the essay step by step from the information amassed.

It is at this point that the student may decide the material indicates that a new or different tack should be taken, that it is advisable to alter the original outline, perhaps drastically, or that he or she was on target right from the start. Whatever the decision, a final outline is cast, the one on which the facts of the research must ultimately hang. And when the dust has cleared, that new outline should contain the main theme, a list of points to be emphasized, and the placement of those points in the finished paper. That paper is now ready to be written.

WRITING THE PAPER

The preceding steps have lead to the actual writing of the first draft of the essay, and there are easily a hundred ways of attacking this task. The simplest is for students to know what they want to say about the topic and then to say it simply and directly. Clarity is important; when the paper is finished, there ought to be no mistaking its intent.

Setting down in order all the material gathered is not enough. The writing must reflect the writer; that is to say, it should be imbued with individual thoughts on the topic, individual questions on the material, and intellectual strength in bringing opposite opinions face to face.

To wind up the demands of form, the student must remember that when quotations, opinions, or statistics are woven into the fabric of the essay, they must be acknowledged through footnotes. Also, the completed paper must contain a title page at the beginning and a bibliography at the end.

FORM OF THE PAPER

To grasp a handy maxim, neatness counts. It would be almost cavalier to spend all the time and energy that a good paper demands and then produce a sloppy, nonuniform, slipshod copy for the instructor.

Usually an instructor requires that the paper have a suitable cover and that its parts be arranged in a logically flowing sequence; a sequence such as the following is generally found acceptable:

I. Title Page. This should be uniformly spaced and must bear the following information:

Title of the paper in capital letters
Student's name
Course designation
School name
Date

II. Preface (optional). This usually acknowledges any debts the writer incurred in researching the topic.

III. Table of Contents. This should be on a separate page and should list the name of each chapter or division, any appendixes used, and the bibliography. Each of these sections is to be identified by the page number where it is to be found. Frequently, a paper is not divided into chapters and contains no index, and so it follows that a table of contents is unnecessary.

IV. Illustrations. If used, these should be listed on a separate page and otherwise treated as the table of contents is treated.

V. The manuscript itself should be neatly typed on one side of white standard 8½ X 11 paper. Corrected typographical errors usually are acceptable, but too many make the product unworthy of the time and work invested. The body of type should be arranged neatly on each page, with plenty of room at the top and bottom and at each margin.

The text should be double-spaced, but single-spaced verse, extended prose quotations, and footnotes are conventional. Should a quote run less than two typewritten lines, quotation marks are used.

Finally, the page numbers, including those of the appendices and bibliography, are marked in arabic numerals in the upper right corner.

VI. Preparing the footnotes and bibliography usually causes the student much grief. The next section, therefore, has been devoted to this area (pp. 40-69).

3

Footnotes and Bibliography

FOOTNOTES

Few aspects of writing cause as much confusion, bewilderment, and frustration as the proper use of footnotes. Footnotes are an essential part of scholarly writing, but until the fundamentals of their use are mastered, the footnote requirement can be a constant source of frustration. As a writing device, footnotes are useful because they allow important information to be communicated without overburdening the text. More specifically, footnotes allow a writer to reflect both credit and blame where they are due by showing the source of facts and ideas, thereby permitting the reader to utilize cited sources. In addition, footnotes act as a helpful context for presented information, indicating sources from which it came—and thus allowing the reader to judge the possible bias of such sources. Finally, footnotes allow a writer to discuss interesting sidelights of the material without breaking the flow of writing.

Two questions invariably arise whenever footnotes are required:

1. What should be footnoted?

2. What form is correct, particularly if unusual or specialized material is being used, such as mimeographed campaign literature?

What To Footnote

While most style manuals or term paper handbooks deal with footnote form, few ever touch upon the more difficult and confusing question of what kind of source should be footnoted and when. There are no ready answers to this question and, unfortunately, it is quite easy to succumb to excess in either direction. If one feels uneasy about an assignment, the material, or the professor's standards and expectations, it is quite tempting to "over-document" a paper or to hang footnotes on it as though one were decorating a Christmas tree. This approach can be hazardous, for besides wasting time, the reader is overburdened with needless side trips to the bottom of the page, and the likelihood of making technical errors is increased. Such errors would, of course, detract from the substance of a paper. Unnecessary footnotes, far from being a safeguard, can become a real problem.

Equally hazardous is the practice of "under-documentation." If footnoting has always been a mystery, something to be avoided, the possibility arises that the material will be distorted: important points may be omitted in order to avoid documentation, or the source of information and ideas may be left to the reader's imagination, implying that the work of others is somehow your own. Between these two unfortunate extremes three styles of scholarship are defined: the original scholar, the scholarly summarizer, and the essayist and journalist. The style that most closely approximates the assigned type of paper should be followed. The *original scholar* form is appropriate for Ph.D. dissertations, Master's theses, honors papers, or term papers that fulfill the major portion of the requirements for a course. This style should also be used for papers consisting mainly of scholarly research from primary sources.

The *scholarly summarizer* style is appropriate for more frequently assigned term papers that fulfill a minor portion of the requirements for a course. This type of paper usually consists of a summary, interpretation, and synthesis of secondary sources.

The *essayist and journalist* style is also appropriate for many types of term papers, but in such cases the emphasis is upon the writer's own experience or interpretation. Strictly speaking, there are few ideas that are completely new; however, if the emphasis is to be on an original and creative reaction to these ideas, and not on the ideas themselves or their origin, the essayist style is appropriate. This style may also be used if the paper is primarily a personal account or a narrative of events witnessed or situations in which the writer participated.

Table 5 summarizes the use of footnotes for each of the styles of scholarship.

QUOTATIONS

There is little question concerning the footnoting of direct quotations. The *original scholar* and the *scholarly summarizer* almost always footnote direct quotations, The exceptions for even the most scholarly styles are quotations from such items of public domain as the Bible and the Constitution. In such cases it is permissible to incorporate a general reference into the text of the material. Form for quotations is covered in the next section.

Example:

There seemed little question that the proposal violated the "equal protection clause," the Fourteenth Amendment to the Constitution.

The dogmatic insistence of the neighborhood leader's position reminded one of Henry Clay's, "Sir, I would rather be right than President."

TABLE 5 / Three Types of Scholarship and Appropriate Footnote Use

Type of Information	Original Scholar	Scholarly Summarizer	Essayist and Journalist
Quotations	All except those quotations of common knowledge, in which case they would still be footnoted if they varied from one edition to another.	Same as original scholar.	Only if the quotation is controversial or highly significant to the text, in which case the reference would be incorporated into the body of the material.
Facts 1. Controversial 2. Significant to the paper 3. Obscure	All but those that are part of common knowledge.	All controversial facts, a representative amount of significant facts to indicate the nature of sources, and only obscure facts that are central to the meaning of the paper.	Only controversial facts central to the meaning of the paper.
Commentary and Interpretation			
Tangential Information	Used frequently for points that might need amplification.	Only for points the absence of which might distort the meaning of the work.	Rarely used except for humor.
Methodology	Brief bibliographical essay showing the scope of material.	Refers to other works that would contain bibliographical essays.	Only if similar methodology would yield significantly different results.
Context of Opinions and Sources	Brief bibliographical essay showing scope of the material.	Refers to other works that would contain bibliographical essays.	Only to indicate that the author is aware of major different approaches; can be incorporated into the text.

The *essayist and journalist* makes even greater use of the device of incorporating general references into the body of the text.

Example:

The writer as a witness or observer: "Sir," Reynaud replied, "we know that you will carry on. We would also if we saw any hope of victory." Winston S. Churchill, *Their Finest Hour, The Second World War* (Boston: Houghton Mifflin, 1949).

FACTS

The *original scholars* footnote all but the most obvious facts. If in doubt they ask themselves if the average mature reader would automatically be aware of the origin and authenticity of a particular fact. If not, it should be footnoted. In general, the three criteria for footnoting facts are

1. *Controversiality*: Could honest men or women disagree over the authenticity or significance of this fact?
2. *Significance* to the paper: Does a significant part of the argument rest upon this fact?
3. *Obscurity*: Are the means or sources for establishing the authenticity of this fact beyond the average reader's experience or recall?

In general, if a fact could be questioned in a scholarly paper on the basis of any of these three criteria, it should be footnoted.

The *scholarly summarizer* needs to footnote only a representative sampling of his significant facts. In this way, the type of sources used is indicated. Obscure facts need not be footnoted unless they are central to the significance of the paper.

The *essayist and journalist* seldom footnotes facts unless they are both controversial and significant to the basic purpose of the paper.

COMMENTARY AND INTERPRETATION

Not every individual will read a report with the same interest. Some readers will be interested only in the main conclusions and the general thread of ideas, while others will be interested in exploring in depth various aspects of the supporting evidence. Other readers will want to read the interesting sidelights found in research; some will find these sidelights a definite distraction. How is it possible for one manuscript to please such widely varying tastes?

Footnotes that comment upon and interpret data can be a partial solution to this dilemma. Such footnotes can be used for supplementary information that will be of interest to some readers. Again, the use of such footnotes varies with the style of scholarship. The *original scholar* does not want to overburden the text with a full explanation of the development of the methodology. In order to fully understand the methodology, it is also important to make the scope of articles in journals or books dealing with this methodology available to the reader. Such an explanation takes the form of the bibliographical footnote.

Example:

Cf. Glendon Schubert, "Ideologies and Attitudes, Academic and Judicial," *Journal of Politics* 29 (February 1967): 3-40; "Academic Ideology and the Study of Adjudication," *Saturday Review* 61 (March 1967): 106-129; I. Howard, Jr., "On the Fluidity of Judicial Choice," *American Political Science Review* 62 (May 1968): 43.

If library rather then empirical research is used, a similar bibliographical footnote dealing with library sources is appropriate.

Example:

> Prominent commentary on political obligations was offered by Thomas Aquinas, Locke, Rousseau, and notably T. H. Green, who may have been the first to use the term. A study of Green's thought and environment is Melvin Richter, *The Politics of Conscience: T. H. Green and His Age* (Cambridge, Mass.: Harvard University Press, 1964), pp. 5-57. Also, review John Plamenatz, *Consent, Freedom, and Political Obligation*, 2nd ed. (New York: Oxford University Press, 1968).

TANGENTIAL INFORMATION

The *original scholar* also can use footnotes to provide tangential information, as in the following:

Examples:

Information Concerned with Research Methodology:

"We exclude respondents who claimed knowledge but are unable to produce a fragment of an accurate observation." Raymond E. Wolfinger and Fred I. Greenstein, "The Repeal of Fair Housing in California," *American Political Science Review* 62 (September 1968): 955.

Meaning of Words:

"The Russian word for election, *vybory*, literally means choices, alternatives." Jerome M. Gilisin, "Soviet Elections as a Measure of Dissent: The Missing One Percent," *American Political Science Review* 62 (September 1968): 85.

Clarifying Information:

"It should be kept in mind that each Soviet voter casts several ballots—as many as seven—so that two million negative votes represent perhaps on the order of 500,000 to 700,000 dissenters." Jerome M. Gilisin, "Soviet Elections as a Measure of Dissent: The Missing One Percent," *American Political Science Review* 62 (September 1968): 816.

Some *essayists* also place tangential material in footnotes as a humorous literary device.

Example:
> " 'Where did you sleep last night and the night before that?' (This last is an essay question, for the air traveler is usually able to declare, in good faith, that he has not slept at all for the past week)." C. Northcote Parkinson, *Parkinson's Law and Other Studies in Administration* (Boston: Houghton Mifflin, 1957), p. 108.

METHODOLOGY AND CONTEXT OF OPINIONS AND SOURCES

Where the *original scholar* uses footnotes to present a short bibliographical essay on his sources, the *scholarly summarizer* uses footnotes to point to the location of such documentation in other sources. This identification of other sources is equally useful for both library and empirical research.

Examples:

Methodological:
For a useful survey of different methods that have been used to analyze roll-call data, see Lee F. Anderson, Meredith W. Watts, Jr., and Allen R. Wilcox, *Legislative Roll-Call Analysis* (Evanston, Ill.: Northwestern University Press, 1966). See also Duncan MacRae, Jr., *Issues and Parties in Legislative Voting: Methods of Statistical Analysis* (New York: Harper & Row, 1970) for a careful and systematic review of the statistical literature relevant to roll-call analysis.

From Stephen J. Brams and Michael K. O'Leary, "An Axiomatic Model of Voting Bodies," *American Political Science Review* 64 (June 1970): 449.

Library Sources:

P. W. Bridgman is generally regarded as the father of the operational philosophy, and his intellectual indebtedness to Bentley is reflected in Bridgman, "Error, Quantum Theory, and the Observer," in *Life, Language, Law: Essays in Honor of Arthur F. Bentley*, ed. Richard W. Taylor (Yellow Springs, Ohio: Antioch Press, 1957), pp. 125-31.

From Steven R. Brown and John Ellithorp, "Emotional Experiences in Political Groups: The Case of the McCarthy Phenomena," *American Political Science Review* 64 (June 1970):349.

Context of Opinions:

For this position, see Richard Wasserstrom, "Disobeying the Law," *The Journal of Philosophy* 58 (1961): 641-53. Also see I. Howard, Jr., "On the Fluidity of Judicial Choice," *American Political Science Review* 62 (1968): 80.

The *scholarly summarizer* thus uses interpretative footnotes to demonstrate an awareness of the broader scope of material, but does not feel compelled to list all of them.

The *essayist and journalist* is much more likely to incorporate such comments and interpretations into the text. However, if the *essayist and journalist* uses a research method, different versions of which yield highly different results, he or she is also compelled to make some justification of the methodology. Such justifications tend to break the flow of writing and, again, can be placed in footnotes.

Example:

"I rely for this version of the Vice-Presidential selection on the excellent and exclusive reporting of Carleton Kent, in the *Chicago Sun-Times*, reporting acknowl-

edged by those who were present to be authentic."
Theodore H. White, *The Making of the President 1960*
(New York: Atheneum, 1961), p. 201.

The same instructions apply to the use of library sources.

Example:
"One of the landmark studies in the field of business
administration is *Strategy and Structure* by A. D.
Chandler, Jr." Lawrence E. Fouraker and John M.
Stopford, "Organization, Structure and the Multination
Strategy," *Administrative Science Quarterly* 13 (1968):
485.

BIBLIOGRAPHY

All three styles of scholarship utilize bibliographies, but
there is a slight variation between the two more scholarly styles
and that of the *essayist and journalist*. Both the *original scholar*
and the *scholarly summarizer* place their bibliographic entries in
categories of written form. The most common are books,
periodicals, newspapers (sometimes combined with periodicals),
government documents, dissertations, unpublished manuscripts,
interviews, and letters. The *essayist and journalist* usually does
not have enough citations to justify separate categories, and
simply lists all sources alphabetically, by the last name of the
author. A bibliography should include all works cited in
footnotes plus any other works that were used. Works that were
examined but not used should not be cited.

FORM

Footnote and bibliography forms are one of the few things
in life in which one can justifiably be arbitrary. There is no
inherent reason to use one form rather than another, except for
the sake of clear communication and consistency. The works
used should be cited in the same form as that used in indexes,

bibliographies, or library card catalogs. In this way, a reader will be able to locate cited sources.

Following are examples of the most frequent types of footnotes and bibliographies used in a political science paper, along with general comments and explanations. Most of the forms are based upon *The University of Chicago Manual of Style*, 12th ed., rev. (Chicago: The University of Chicago Press, 1969). The Chicago manual does not specifically cover several forms, such as interviews and political pamphlets, that are likely to be used by students of political science. In such cases, examples given are consistent with Kate L. Turabian, *Student Guide for Writing College Papers*, 2nd ed., rev. (Chicago: The University of Chicago Press, 1969). The legal citations are based upon *A Uniform System of Citation*, 11th ed., *Harvard Law Review*, 1968.

FOOTNOTES, GENERAL RULES

Books should include:

1. Author's full name
2. Complete title
3. Editor, compiler, or translator (if any)
4. Name of series, volume or series number (if any)
5. Number of volumes
6. City, publisher, and date
7. Volume number and page number

Articles should include:

1. Author
2. Title of article
3. Periodical
4. Volume of periodical
5. Date and page numbers of article

Unpublished material should include:

1. Author
2. Title (if any)

3. Type of material
4. Where it may be found
5. Date
6. Page number (if any)

Bibliography, General Rules

Footnote style can be changed into bibliographic style by transposing author's first and last names, removing parentheses from facts of publication, omitting page references, and repunctuating with periods instead of commas.

Books should include:

1. Name of author(s), editors, or institutions responsible
2. Full title, including subtitle if one exists
3. Series (if any)
4. Volume number
5. Editions, if not the original
6. Publisher's name (sometimes omitted)
7. Date of publication

Articles should include:

1. Name of author
2. Title of article
3. Name of periodical
4. Volume number (or date, or both)
5. Pages

Book with One Author

Footnote: 2. George Sabine, *A History of Political Theory* (New York: Holt, Rinehart & Winston, 1961), pp. 467-68.

Bibliography: Sabine, George. *A History of Political Theory.* New York: Holt, Rinehart & Winston, 1961.

Comments: Titles of other works appearing in the title are in quotation marks.

Book with Two Authors

Footnote: 3. Robert Dahl and Charles Lindblom, *Politics, Economics, and Welfare* (New York: Harper & Row, 1953), p. 115.

Bibliography: Dahl, Robert, and Lindblom, Charles. *Politics, Economics, and Welfare.* New York: Harper & Row, 1953.

Book with Three Authors

Footnote: 4. John R. Meyer, John F. Kain, and Martin Wohl, *The Urban Transportation Problem* (Cambridge, Mass.: Harvard University Press, 1968), p. 50.

Bibliography: Meyer, John; Kain, John F.; and Wohl, Martin. *The Urban Transportation Problem.* Cambridge, Mass.: Harvard University Press, 1968.

Book with More Than Three Authors

Footnote: 5. John Wahlke et al., *The Legislative System* (New York: John Wiley & Sons, 1962), p. 23.

Bibliography: Wahlke, John; Eulau, Heinz; Buchanan, William; and Ferguson, LeRoy C. *The Legislative System.* New York: John Wiley & Sons, 1962.

Book with an Association as Author

Footnote: 33. National Manpower Council, *Government and Manpower* (New York: Columbia University Press, 1964), p. 76.

Bibliography: National Manpower Council. *Government and Manpower.* New York: Columbia University Press, 1964.

Pseudonym, Author's Real Name Known

Footnote: 35. Samuel Clemens [Mark Twain], *Huckleberry*

Finn (New York: Harcourt, Brace & World, 1969), p. 8.

Bibliography: Clemens, Samuel [Mark Twain]. *Huckleberry Finn*. New York: Harcourt, Brace & World, 1969.

Author's Name Not on Title Page, but Known

Footnote: 7. [Alexander Hamilton, James Madison, and John Jay], *The Federalist Papers*, ed. Jacob Cook (Middletown, Conn.: Wesleyan University Press, 1961), p. 182.

Bibliography: [Hamilton, Alexander; Madison, James; and Jay, John.] *The Federalist Papers*. Edited by Jacob Cook. Middletown, Conn.: Wesleyan University Press, 1961.

Book's Author Anonymous

Footnote: 6. *The Holy Quran* (Washington, D.C.: Islamic Center, 1960), p. 177.

Bibliography: *The Holy Quran*. Washington, D.C.: Islamic Center, 1960.
Comments: Avoid use of "Anon." or "Anonymous."

Book by Editor, Compiler, or Translator: No Other Author Listed

Editors

Footnote: 8 Robert Theobold, ed., *Social Policies for America in the Seventies: Nine Divergent Views* (New York: Doubleday, 1968), p. 85.

Bibliography: Theobold, Robert, ed. *Social Policies for America in the Seventies: Nine Divergent Views*. New York: Doubleday, 1968.

Compilers

Footnote: 9. Robert Lindsay and John Neu, comps., *French Political Pamphlets, 1547-1648* (Madison: University of Wisconsin Press, 1969), p. 8.

Bibliography: Lindsay, Robert, and Neu, John, comps. *French Political Pamphlets, 1547-1648*. Madison: University of Wisconsin Press, 1969.

Translators

Footnote: 10. Ursule Molinaro, trans., *Beowulf* (New York: Farrar, Straus & Giroux, 1957), p. 23.

Bibliography: Molinaro, Ursule, trans. *Beowulf.* New York: Farrar, Straus & Giroux, 1957.

Translated or Edited Book in Which the Author Is Known

Footnote: 20. Gustav Stolper, Karl Hauser, and Knut Borchardt, *The German Economy, 1870 to Present*, trans. Toni Stoper (New York: Harcourt, Brace & World, 1969), pp. 8-10.

Bibliography: Stolper, Gustav; Hauser, Karl; and Borchardt, Knut. *The German Economy, 1870 to Present*. Translated by Toni Stoper. New York: Harcourt, Brace & World, 1969.

Edited or Translated Work in Which the Editor Is More Important than the Author

Footnote: 11. William L. Riordon, ed. *Plunkitt of Tammany Hall*, by George Washington Plunkitt (New York: E. P. Dutton, 1900), p. 25.

Bibliography: Riordon, William L., ed. *Plunkitt of Tammany Hall*, by George Washington Plunkitt. New York: E. P. Dutton, 1900.

Book, Multivolume

Footnote: 23. Fred E. Inbau, James R. Thompson, and Claude
R. Sowle, *Cases and Comments on Criminal Justice*,
3 vols. (Mineola, N.Y.: Foundation Press, 1969),
1:5.

Bibliography: Inbau, Fred E.; Thompson, James R.; Sowle,
Claude R. *Cases and Comments on Criminal
Justice*. Vol. 1. Mineola, N.Y.: Foundation
Press, 1969.

Book in a Series

Footnote: 2. W. F. Gutteridge, *The Military in African Politics*,
Studies in African History (London: Methuen,
1969), p. 22.

Bibliography: Gutteridge, W. F. *The Military in African Politics*. Studies in African History. London:
Methuen, 1969.

Comments: If a book is part of a series, the citation should
include the name of the series and the volume number. Spell
out the author's name in full unless he is commonly known by
his initials, e.g., W. F. Gutteridge.

Book in a Series, One Author, Several Volumes, Each with a Different Title

Footnote: 36. Charles Edward Mallet, *The Medieval University
and Colleges Founded in the Middle Ages*, 3 vols.,
The History of Oxford University (New York:
Barnes & Noble, 1968), 1:23.

Bibliography: Mallet, Charles Edward. *The Medieval University
and Colleges Founded in the Middle Ages*. Vol.
1. The History of Oxford University. New
York: Barnes & Noble, 1968.

Paperback Edition of a Book
First Published in Hard Cover

Footnote: 22. Aaron Wildavsky, *The Politics of the Budgetary Process* (Boston: Little, Brown, paperback, 1964), p. 177.

Bibliography: Wildavsky, Aaron. *The Politics of the Budgetary Process.* Paperback. Boston: Little, Brown, 1964.

Introduction to Book by Another Author

Footnote: 34. Alex Inkeles, Introduction to *The Process of Modernization*, by John Brode (Cambridge, Mass.: Harvard University Press, 1969), p. vii.

Bibliography: Inkeles, Alex. Introduction to *The Process of Modernization*, by John Brode. Cambridge, Mass.: Harvard University Press, 1969.

Citation in One Book from Another Book

Footnote: 42. Jakob Hegemann, *Entlarvte Geschichte*, p. 210. As quoted in John W. Wheeler-Bennett, *The Nemesis of Power* (London: Macmillan, 1954), p. 8.

Bibliography: Wheeler-Bennett, John W. *The Nemesis of Power.* London: Macmillan, 1954.

Book Review

Footnote: 38. Willard Ranger, "International Politics, Law, and Organization," Review of *Regionalism and World Order*, by Ronald Yalem, *American Political Science Review* 60 (September 1966): 759.

Bibliography: Ranger, Willard. "International Politics, Law, and Organization." Review of *Regionalism and World Order*, by Ronald Yalem. *American Political Science Review* 60 (September 1966): 759.

Literature

Plays and Long Poems
Footnote: 57. George Bernard Shaw, *The Devil's Advocate*, act 2, sc. 1, lines 8-11.

Bibliography: Shaw, George Bernard. *The Devil's Advocate.*

Short Poems
Footnote: 58. Edgar Allan Poe, "To Helen," *Eternal Passion in English Poetry* (Freeport, N.Y.: Books for Libraries, 1969), lines 3-5.

Bibliography: Poe, Edgar Allan. "To Helen." *Eternal Passion in English Poetry.* Freeport, N.Y.: Books for Libraries, 1969.

Bible

Footnote: 14. 1 Ruth 12:18.

Bibliography: 1. *Book of Ruth* 12:18.

Classical Works

Footnote: 15. Julius Caesar, *The Conquest of Gaul* 1., 3-5.

Bibliography: Caesar, Julius. *The Conquest of Gaul* 1.

Modern Edition of Classical Work

Footnote: 4. Augustine, *City of God*, trans. Healey-Tasker 20.3.

Bibliography: Augustine. *City of God*. Translated by Healey-Tasker.

Article, Chapter, or Other Part of a Book

Footnote: 16. Leonard D. White, "The Role of the City Manager," *Urban Government*, rev. ed., edited by

Edward C. Banfield (New York: The Free Press, 1969), p. 286.

Bibliography: White, Leonard D. "The Role of the City Manager," *Urban Government*. Rev. ed. Edited by Edward C. Banfield. New York: The Free Press, 1969.

Works Available in Microfilm

Footnote: 18. Abraham Tauber, *Spelling Reform in the United States* (Ann Arbor, Mich.: University Microfilms, 1958).

Bibliography: Tauber, Abraham. *Spelling Reform in the United States*. Ann Arbor, Mich.: University Microfilms, 1958.

Encyclopedias, Almanacs, and Other Reference Works

Signed Articles
Footnote: 24. *International Encyclopedia of the Social Sciences*, 5th ed., s.v. "Systems Analysis: Political Systems," by William C. Mitchell.

Bibliography: *International Encyclopedia of the Social Sciences*. 5th ed., s.v. "Systems Analysis: Political Systems," by William C. Mitchell.

Unsigned Articles
Footnote: 25. *Oxford Dictionary of National Biography*, s.v. "Akers-Douglas, Aretas."

Bibliography: *Oxford Dictionary of National Biography*. s.v. "Akers-Douglas, Aretas."

Periodical: Author Given

Consecutive Pages
Footnote: 32. David Fellman, "Constitutional Law in 1958-

1959," *American Political Science Review* 54 (1960): 168-70.

Bibliography: Fellman, David. "Constitutional Law in 1958-1959." *American Political Science Review* 54 (1960): 168-70.

Nonconsecutive Pages
Footnote: 33. Will Lissner, "Protection of the Author's Reprint Rights," *American Journal of Economics* 28 (April 1969): 2, 11.

Bibliography: Lissner, Will. "Protection of the Author's Reprint Rights." *American Journal of Economics* 28 (April 1969): 2, 11.

Magazine Article, No Author Given

Footnote: 39. "Tax Changes for 1971: The Plans Take Shape," *U.S. News & World Report*, 5 October 1970, p. 91.

Bibliography: "Tax Changes for 1971: The Plans Take Shape." *U.S. News & World Report*, 5 October 1970, p. 91.

Newspapers

American
Footnote: 12. George C. Wilson, "Copter Force Hits Camp Near Hanoi," *The Washington Post*, 24 November 1970, p. 1A.

Bibliography: Wilson, George C. "Copter Force Hits Camp Near Hanoi." *The Washington Post*, 24 November 1970, p. 1A.

Foreign
Footnote: 13. *Times* (London), 1 December 1970, p. 10.

Bibliography: *Times*. London. 1 December 1970. p. 10.
Comments: Include name of city for foreign newspapers.

Proceedings of a Meeting or Conference: Reproduced

Footnote: 23. The Seventy-seventh Annual Conference of the International Chiefs of Police, "Proceedings of the Conference of the International Chiefs of Police," mimeographed (Atlantic City: C.I.C.P., October 6, 1970), p. 2.

Bibliography: The Seventy-seventh Annual Conference of the International Chiefs of Police. "Proceedings of the Conference of the International Chiefs of Police." Atlantic City: C.I.C.P., October 6, 1970. Mimeographed.

Minutes of a Meeting: Not Reproduced

Footnote: 69. Capitol Improvement Advisory Committee, "Minutes of Meeting of Capitol Improvement Advisory Committee," (Washington, D.C., 5 May 1971), p. 2.

Bibliography: Capitol Improvement Advisory Committee. "Minutes of Meeting of Capitol Improvement Advisory Committee." Washington, D.C., 5 May 1971.

Paper Read or Speech Delivered at a Meeting

Footnote: 12. John N. Mitchell, "Legalized Wiretapping" (Address delivered at the Seventy-seventh Annual Conference of International Chiefs of Police, Atlantic City, October 5, 1970), p. 5.

Bibliography: Mitchell, John N. "Legalized Wiretapping." Address delivered at the Seventy-seventh Annual Conference of International Chiefs of Police, October 5, 1970, at Atlantic City.

Thesis or Dissertation

Footnote: 25. William John Thomson, "Variables Affecting

Human Discrimination Processes" (Ph.D. dissertation, Stanford University, 1969), p. 87.

Bibliography: Thomson, William John. "Variables Affecting Human Discrimination Processes." Ph.D. dissertation, Stanford University, 1969.

Legal Citations

Federal Statute

Footnote: 26. *Administrative Procedure Act*, @ 11-6 U.S.C. @ 1009 (1964).

Bibliography: *Administrative Procedure Act*. @ 11-6 U.S.C. @ 1009 (1964).

State Statute

Footnote: 27. *Blue Sky Law*, @ 2 New York General Business Code @ 352, (McKinney, 1962).

Bibliography: *Blue Sky Law*. @ 2 New York General Business Code @ 352, McKinney, 1962.

Court Case

Footnote: 28. Ker v. California, 357 U.S. 50. (1963).

Bibliography: Ker v. California. 357 U.S. 50 (1963).

Law Review Articles

Footnote: 29. Ebb, *The Grundig-Consten Case Revisited*, 115 Univ. Penn. L. Rev., 885 (1969).

Bibliography: Ebb. *The Grundig-Consten Case Revisited*. 115 Univ. Penn. L. Rev., 1969.

Statutory Material

Footnote: 30. U.S., *Constitution*, Art. 2, sec. 1.

Bibliography: U.S. *Constitution*. Art. 2, sec. 1.

Material from Manuscript Collections

Footnote: 31. Diary of Lewis Tappan, 25 February 1836 to 29 August 1838, Tappan Papers, Library of Congress, Washington, D.C.

Bibliography: Washington, D.C. Library of Congress. Diary of Lewis Tappan, 25 February 1836 to 29 August 1838. Tappan Papers.

Radio and Television Programs

Footnote: 40. CBS , *CBS Evening News*, 8 December 1970, "Rube Goldberg Dies," Walter Cronkite, reporter.

Bibliography: CBS. *CBS Evening News*. 8 December 1970. "Rube Goldberg Dies." Walter Cronkite, reporter.

Interview

Footnote: 41. Interview with Mr. Carl Rauh, Deputy Attorney General for the District of Columbia, Washington, D.C., December 2, 1970.

Bibliography: Interview with Mr. Carl Rauh, Deputy Attorney General for the District of Columbia. Washington, D.C., December 2, 1970.

Mimeographed or Other Nonprinted Reports

Footnote: 13. American University, "Codebook: Baker Survey of Local Elected Officials," mimeographed (Washington, D.C.: American University School of Government), p. 5.

Bibliography: American University. "Codebook: Baker Survey of Local Elected Officials." Washington, D.C.: American University School of Government.

Pamphlet

Footnote: 59. Harold T. Effer, "Joseph Clark, Your Man in Washington," Office of Sen. Clark (Washington, D.C., Fall 1968), p. 2.

Bibliography: Effer, Harold T. "Joseph Clark, Your Man in Washington." Office of Sen. Clark. Washington, D.C., Fall 1968.

Letters

Footnote: 68. Lawrence to Barr, 8 November 1958, Political Papers of Governor David Leo Lawrence, Hillman Library, University of Pittsburgh, Pittsburgh, Pa.

Bibliography: Pittsburgh, Pa. Hillman Library, University of Pittsburgh. Political Papers of Governor David Leo Lawrence. Lawrence to Barr, 8 November 1958.

Documents

Citing documents is always a difficult problem, for their form is totally unlike that of books and magazines. The card catalog is a good guide and the following general rules should help. Include in this order:

1. The country (United States, etc.)
2. The branch of government (legislative, executive, etc.)
3. The subbranch or subbranches (House, Committee on Education and Labor, etc.)

The branches or subbranches can become complicated: a careful examination of the document itself, its entry in the card catalog, or the *United States Government Manual* (see page 130) should give you an idea as to the sequence of organization.

This information is followed by the title (underlined), the name of the series or sequence, and the facts of publication. The following examples include the most commonly cited government publications.

Congressional Documents

Bills

Footnote: 45. U.S., Congress, House, *Higher Education Act of 1965*, H.R. 9567, 89th Cong., 1st sess. 1965, p. 37.

Bibliography: U.S. Congress. House. *Higher Education Act of 1965*. H.R. 9567, 89th Cong., 1st sess., 1965.

Footnote: 46. U.S., Congress, Senate, *Metropolitan Planning Act*, S. 855, 88th Cong., 2nd sess., 1964.

Bibliography: U.S. Congress. Senate. *Metropolitan Planning Act*. S. 855, 88th Cong., 2nd sess., 1964.

Debates

Footnotes: 47. U.S., Congress, Senate, *Congressional Record*, 91st Cong., 2nd sess., 1970, 25, pt. 511: 665.

Bibliography: U.S. Congress. Senate. *Congressional Record*. 91st Congress, 2nd sess., 1970. 25, 511:665.

Report

Footnote: 48. U.S., Congress, House, *Higher Education Act of 1965*, H. Rept. 621 to accompany H.R. 9567, 89th Cong., 1st sess., 1965.

Bibliography: U.S. Congress. House. *Higher Education Act of 1965*. H.R. 9567. 89th Cong., 1st sess., 1965.

Hearings

Footnote: 49. U.S., Congress, House, Committee on Ways and Means, Hearings to exclude from the gross income the first $750 of interest received on deposits in thrift institutions, H.R. 16545, 91st Cong., 2nd sess., 1970.

Bibliography: U.S. Congress. House. Committee on Ways and Means. Hearings to exclude from the gross income the first $750 of interest received on deposits in thrift institutions. H.R. 16545. 91st Cong., 2nd sess. 1970.

Executive Documents

From an Executive Department

Footnote: 43. U.S., Department of Interior, *Final Report to the President on the Potomac Basin: "The Nation's River"* (Washington, D.C.: U.S. Dept. of Interior, 1968), p. 6.

Bibliography: U.S. Department of Interior. *Final Report to the President on the Potomac Basin: "The Nation's River."* Washington, D.C.: U.S. Dept. of Interior, 1968.

Presidential Papers

Footnote: 44. U.S., President, "Statement by the President on Actions and Recommendations for the Federal City, January 31, 1969," *Weekly Compilation of Presidential Documents*, vol. 5, no. 5, February 3, 1970, p. 198.

Bibliography: U.S. President. "Statement by the President on Actions and Recommendations for the Federal City, January 31, 1969." *Weekly Compilation of Presidential Documents.* February 3, 1970.

International Documents

International Organizations

Footnote: 49. League of Nations, Secretariat, *Administration of Territory* (O.J.) (March 1920), p. 52.

Bibliography: League of Nations. Secretariat. *Administration of Territory* (O.J.) (March 1920), p. 52.

Footnote: 51. United Nations, General Assembly, November 20, 1959, *General Assembly Resolution 1386*, A/4353, Annex 16, pp. 19-21.

Bibliography: United Nations. General Assembly. 14th Session, November 20, 1959. *General Assembly Resolution 1386*, A/4353.

Treaties

Footnote: 52. U.S., *Statutes at Large* 43, pt. 2 (December 1923-March 1925), "Naval Arms Limitation Treaty," February 26, 1922, ch. 1, art. 1, p. 1655.

Bibliography: U.S. *Statutes at Large* 43, pt. 2 (December 1923-March 1925). "Naval Arms Limitation Treaty," February 26, 1922.

State and Local Documents

State

Footnote: 57. New Jersey, Office of the Governor, Governor's Select Commission on Civil Disorder, *Report for Action* (Trenton: Office of the Governor, 1968), p. 14.

Bibliography: New Jersey. Office of the Governor. Governor's Select Commission on Civil Disorder. *Report for Action*. Trenton: Office of the Governor, 1968.

City

Footnote: 58. New York, N.Y., Mayor's Office, Mayor's Task Force on Reorganization of New York City Government, *The Mayor's Task Force on Reorganization of New York City Government: Report and Proposed Local Law* (New York: Institute of Public Administration, 1966), p. 9.

Bibliography: New York, N.Y. Mayor's Office. Mayor's Task

Force on Reorganization of New York City Government. *The Mayor's Task Force on Reorganization of New York City Government: Report and Proposed Local Law*. New York: Institute of Public Administration, 1966.

SECOND OR LATER REFERENCES TO FOOTNOTES

Chances are several references will be made to the same footnote. The general rules are as follows:

1. For references to the same work with no intervening footnotes simply use the Latin term "ibid.," meaning "in the same place."
2. For second references with no intervening footnote, but with a different page of the same work, state Ibid. and the page number.
EXAMPLE: Ibid., p. 87.
3. For second references with intervening footnotes, state: the author's last name, but not first name or initials unless another author of the same name is cited; a shortened title of the work; and the specific page number.

Following are examples of second citations of a representative number of works.

Second References with Intervening Citations

Book, Single Volume
First Citation: 1. Thomas E. Skidmore, *Politics in Brazil* (New York: Oxford University Press, 1967), p. 81.

Second Citation: 8. Skidmore, *Politics in Brazil*, p. 92.

Multivolume
First Citation: 2. Fred E. Inbau, James R. Thomas, and Claude R. Sowle, *Cases and Comments on Criminal*

Justice, 3 vols. (Mineola, N.Y.: Foundation Press, 1968) 1:5.

Second Citation: 9. Inbau, Thomas, and Sowle, *Cases and Comments*, 1:8.

Article in Anthology

First Citation: 3. Ronald Cohen, "Anthropology and Political Science: Courtship and Marriage?" *Politics and the Social Sciences*, ed. Seymour M. Lipset (New York: Oxford University Press, 1969), p. 22.

Second Citation: 10. Cohen, "Anthropology and Political Science," p. 23.

Journal Article

First Citation: 4. David Fellman, "Constitutional Law in 1958-1959," *American Political Science Review* 54 (1960): 168.

Second Citation: 11. Fellman, "Constitutional Law," p. 171.

Book with an Editor or Translator, Author Unknown

First Citation: 5. Robert Theobold, ed., *Social Policies for America in the Seventies: Nine Divergent Views* (Garden City, N.Y.: Doubleday, 1968), p. 3.

Second Citation: 12. Robert Theobold, ed., *Social Policies in the Seventies*, p. 4.

Classical

First Citation: 6. Thucydides, *History of the Peloponnesian Wars*, 2.30, 2.

Second Citation: 13. Thucy., 2.28, 1-6.

Letters

First Citation: 7. Stevens to Sumner, 28 August 1865, Charles

                  Sumner Papers, Harvard College Library, Cambridge, Mass.

Second Citation: 14. Stevens to Sumner, 28 August 1865.

State Documents
First Citation: 15. Maryland, *Ordinance Number 438*, (1965) sec. 8.

Second Citation: 17. Maryland, *Ordinance Number 438*, sec. 8.

Federal Document
First Citation: 16. U.S., *Statutes at Large* 43, pt. 2 (Dec. 1923-March 1925), "Naval Arms Limitation Treaty," Feb. 26, 1922, ch. 1, art. 1, p. 1655.

Second Citation: 18. U.S., *Statutes at Large* 43, "Naval Arms Limitation Treaty," p. 1655.

PART TWO

4

Annotated Listing of Basic References

Information relevant to political science is organized in a variety of ways. Some information focuses upon particular subjects—such as individual political events, laws, etc. These sources contain a wide variety of information centering on a particular subject. The *Congressional Quarterly,* for instance, which includes a wide variety of different forms, information, statistics, prose, theories, etc., is nevertheless concerned entirely with laws, policies, and programs. In contrast, some sources specialize in a particular kind of information—that is, statistics, public opinion data, definitions of terms—about a wide variety of subjects in the field of politics. See, for example, the collected Gallup Polls, which cover virtually every aspect of government and politics plus a number of other areas. This section is divided into two main parts: forms of information and subjects of information. Additional sections are also provided covering action guides for the political process and other research guides.

FORMS OF INFORMATION

Abstracts and Digests

African Abstracts. London: International African Institute, 1950–.

A quarterly journal, this work offers summaries of scholarly articles on Africa; they cover such topics as "Classifying African Political Parties" and "Urbanization and Social Change in Africa." It contains a useful index.

The American Political Process. Dwight L. Smith and Lloyd W. Garrison, eds. Santa Barbara, Calif.: ABC-Clio, 1972.

This contains incisive abstracts of key articles organized in refined categories. A characteristic article might list twenty article abstracts on ethnic voting in America.

Current Digest of the Soviet Press. The American Association for the Advancement of Slavic Studies. Columbus, Ohio: Ohio State University, 1929–.

Next to being there, this publication is considered one of the best ways to study the Soviet Union. Published weekly, it contains American translations of all the major documents and significant articles from about sixty Soviet newspapers and magazines plus a complete index to the two principal dailies, *Pravda* and *Izvestia.* The translations are without comment or even interpretation but are excellent raw material for critical analysis. A detailed quarterly index is also published as is a new monthly, *Current Abstracts of the Soviet Press,* offering, obviously, the monthly highlights of Soviet news with emphasis on internal discussion.

Environment Abstracts. New York: Environment Information Center, 1974.

While slanted toward scientific material, these abstracts, published monthly, will enable the political science researcher to develop a grasp of the work in a highly specialized area.

International Political Science Abstracts. Oxford: Basil Black-well, 1951–.

Prepared quarterly by the International Political Science Association and the International Studies Conference, with the support of the Coordination Committee on Documentation in the Social Sciences, each volume contains about 350 abstracts, including 150 abstracted journals. In the first volume, a very broad subject group is covered, with author and subject indexes. Subsequently, the arrangement is alphabetical by author, with cumulated subject and author indexes in the fourth issue of each year. Abstracts of articles in English are in English; those articles in other languages are translated into French only.

Peace Research Abstracts Journal. Clarkson, Ontario: Canadian Peace Research Institute, 1964–.

This monthly journal offers extensive abstracts of books and articles directly or remotely associated with peace. Its topical organization is useful for suggesting research ideas.

Poverty and Human Resources Abstracts. Ann Arbor: Institute of Labor and Industrial Relations, University of Michigan and Wayne State University, Sage, 1966–.

This bimonthly work contains abstracts of articles in such politically related areas as urban change, living standards, education, and housing.

Psychological Abstracts. Washington: American Psychological Association, 1927.

These are abstracts in the area of motivation, social psychology, group behavior, and other cross-disciplinary topics.

Research Annual on Intergroup Relations. Melvin Tumin and Barbara Anderson. Chicago: Quadrangle Books, 1970–.

Many political conflicts are reflections of group conflicts—American racial and religious conflicts, Arab and Israeli conflicts, Catholics versus Protestants, conflicts of French- and

English-speaking residents of Canada. This source presents brief abstracts of all the important research on intergroup conflict each year. Articles are grouped according to the type of conflict discussed—racial, religious, linguistic, etc.

Sociological Abstracts. New York: Sociological Abstracts, 1952–.

In recent years many concepts and ideas in political science have come from sociology. The idea of a social system originated with sociologist Talcott Parsons. Bureaucracy, socialization, public opinion, and many other "political" concepts are dealt with in sociological journals. These abstracts are divided into approximately twenty subsections and could be quite helpful in many areas.

Bibliographies

GENERAL BIBLIOGRAPHIES

Below are listed several general indexing and bibliographic guides. They cover a broad range but can provide bibliographies in a variety of areas within each field. The strength of these guides is their scope. A source for your topic can probably be found in one of these guides although probably not in a particular spot. Their difficulty is also related to their broad scope. You must learn how to use each and discover the various ways in which your topic might be categorized.

ABS Guide to Recent Publications in the Social and Behavioral Sciences. Beverly Hills, Calif.: The American Behavioral Scientist, Sage, 1965–.

Drawing from over four hundred monthly publications in sociology, anthropology, psychology, public policy, and political science, this guide identifies the most interesting articles in a variety of areas. (If you are interested in the psychological reasons behind a particular voting trend, for instance, this guide will identify new articles in this area.)

Bibliographic Index. New York: H. W. Wilson, 1937—.

This master source for bibliographies lists bibliographies published separately as well as those found in books, pamphlets, and periodicals. It is published semiannually.

Cumulative Book Index. New York: H. W. Wilson, 1898—.

This monthly index with cumulations provides a comprehensive list of all new books published in various areas of interest, some of which might not be found in a college library, and usually lists the other works by each author published within the time span covered. Also of value to the researcher is a selected list of important government documents that is included in the index. Since 1925 the *Cumulative Book Index* has included books in the English language that are published outside the United States. Books are listed by author, title, and subject.

International Bibliography of Political Science. The International Committee for Social Sciences Documentation. Chicago: Aldine, 1962—.

These annual volumes contain a select worldwide list of the most important books and articles in political science. The topics are often highly specialized.

International Bibliography of Political Science. Vols. 1-8, Paris: UNESCO, Vol. 9, Chicago: Aldine, 1952—.

This reference work has been published annually since 1952 by the International Committee for Social Sciences Documentation under the auspices of the International Political Science Association. As the title suggests, it includes an international selection of the most important publications in the discipline.

Political Science Bibliographies. Robert B. Harmon. Metuchen, N.J.: Scarecrow, 1973.

This book contains nearly eight hundred entries listing many bibliographies in the field.

Universal Reference System. Political Science, Government, and Public Policy Series. N.J.: Princeton Research, 1969.

This source consists of a ten-volume set of references with annual supplements. It will take approximately twenty minutes to master the unique computerized index system of this source; once done, specialized high-quality bibliographies are available. Each of the volumes covers a major area of political science such as international affairs, legislative decision making, administrative management, law, jurisprudence, and judicial process. Each lists and summarizes thousands of books, articles, papers, and documents selected by the leading political scholars of our day.

BIBLIOGRAPHIES IN SPECIAL SUBJECT AREAS

Following are select bibliographies in key areas of current interest. This is an *illustrative* list; its purpose is not to cover the whole area of political science but to illustrate the kinds of bibliographies available.

American Government and Politics

Alternatives in Print, The Annual Catalogue of Social Change. Compiled by American Library Association. Columbus, Ohio: Ohio State University Libraries, 1973.

This is a guide to a wide range of political movements and their publications. Organizations are indexed by subject, and each entry includes publications, price lists, and information for ordering. Contrary to the title, it has not been published annually.

Amnesty in America: An Annotated Bibliography. Morris Sherman. Passaic, N.J.: New Jersey Library Association, 1974.

While this publication does not include President Ford's proclamation, citations go back to 1790 on all aspects of the amnesty question.

Attitude Change: A Review and Bibliography of Selected Research. Earl E. Davis. Paris: UNESCO, 1964.

An analytic bibliographic essay on the various kinds of research behind attitude change.

Confrontation, Conflict, and Dissent: A Bibliography of a Decade of Controversy, 1960-1970. Albert Jay Miller. Metuchen, N.J.: Scarecrow, 1972.

While not annotated, the citations are numerous and arranged in topical chapters, covering general information, student dissent, firearms, etc.

Housing and Planning References. United States Department of Housing and Urban Development. Washington, D.C.: Government Printing Office, 1948–.

This bimonthly publication selects key books and articles in a variety of politically related areas such as zoning, pollution, crime and law enforcement, noise control, and low-income housing.

The Literature of Isolationism: A Guide to Non-Interventionist Scholarship, 1930-1972. Justus D. Doenecke. Colorado Springs, Colo.: Ralph Myles, 1972.

In the form of an extensive bibliographical essay, this book covers scholarship suggesting that a nation (the United States) should remain uninvolved with the rest of the world.

Political Campaign Communication: A Bibliography and Guide to the Literature. Lynda Lee Kaid, Keith R. Sanders, and Robert O. Hirsch. Metuchen, N.J.: Scarecrow, 1974.

This includes entries relevant to the communications process as it operated in a political campaign or similar contest in the United States from 1950 to 1972. It is specialized, but the beginning student can easily become interested in such works as James Powell, "Reactions to John F. Kennedy's Delivery Skills in the 1960 Campaign," *Western Speech,* 1968.

Poverty in the United States During the Sixties. Dorothy Campbell Tompkins. Berkeley, Calif.: Institute for Government Studies, University of California, 1970.

The 1960s witnessed a "war on poverty." This huge volume outlines the massive research accompanying the anti-poverty effort. Arranged by topic with limited annotations, it is action oriented: Who are the poor? Where do they live? What is being done for the poor?

The Role of Political Parties in Congress: A Bibliography and Research Guide. Charles O. Jones and Randall B. Ripley. Tucson: University of Arizona Press, 1966.

While specialized and relatively short, this bibliography does serve as a study guide describing how to locate and use documents, subjects for study, etc.

Selection of the Vice-President. Dorothy Campbell Tompkins. Berkeley, Calif.: Institute of Governmental Studies, University of California, 1974.

This work includes history as well as quotations and suggestions for change.

Selected Bibliography on State Government 1959-1972. Lexington, Ky.: Council on State Governments, 1972.

This book uses author and key-word indexes. It is oriented toward practical problems and official reports rather than academic treatment.

The Study and Analysis of Black Politics: A Bibliography. Hanes Walton, Jr. Metuchen, N.J.: Scarecrow, 1973.

This book contains useful introductory essays on the variety and scope of writings on the Black political experience. The extensive listings are not annotated but are arranged topically, i.e., Black political candidate, Black pressure groups, etc.

The Study of Community Power: A Bibliographic Review. Willis D. Hawley and James H. Svara. Santa Barbara, Calif.: ABC-Clio, 1972.

This is a bibliographic essay at its best. It emphasizes the theoretical and methodological issues involved in the study of community power and has extensive annotation.

From Radical Left to Extreme Right. 2nd ed. Theodore Jurgen Spahn, Janet M. Spahn, and Robert H. Muller. Metuchen, N.J.: Scarecrow, 1972.

This is a bibliography of current periodicals of protest with content summaries and publisher feedback to guide the prospective researcher. In addition to the conventional political terminology such as right, left, etc., this useful guide describes a wide spectrum of publications (underground, gay liberation, sexual freedom, race supremacist, metaphysical, UFO, etc.). The content summaries make it a useful guide to political activism in America.

Public Administration: A Bibliography. Howard E. McCurdy. Washington, D.C.: American University, 1972.

This work contains an essay on the development of the field, abstracts of the most frequently cited books in the field, and citations arranged by topic.

Urban Affairs Bibliography. An Annotated Guide to the Literature of the Field. Bernard H. Ross and A. Lee Fritschler. Washington, D.C.: American University, 1974.

A large proportion of the citations in this bibliography are annotated. Its emphasis is political but includes citations from other social sciences, too. The citations are broken down into conventional categories such as urban government and structure, urban policy, housing, education, etc. Of special interest is a directory of urban interest groups in Washington.

Foreign Policy and International Relations
American Defense Policy Since 1945: A Preliminary Bibliography. John Greenwood, ed. National Security Education Program. Lawrence, Kan.: University Press of Kansas, 1973.

This work contains over three thousand items with a detailed table of contents.

Foreign Affairs Bibliography: A Selected and Annotated List of Books on International Relations. Council on Foreign Affairs. New York: R. R. Bowker, 1962.

This is actually a ready-made bibliography on even the most specialized foreign policy topics of the United States and other nations. Organized nation by nation as well as by topic, it contains such subheadings as Liberalism, Conservatism, Colonial Problems, Labor Movements, Human Rights, and the Cold War, and brief annotations that include books, research series, and documents.

Foreign Affairs 50 Year Bibliography: New Evaluations of Significant Books on International Relations 1920-1970. Byron Dexter, ed. Council on Foreign Relations. New York: R. R. Bowker, 1972.

Each decade the influential *Journal of Foreign Affairs* publishes important bibliographies and review books on world affairs. This is a reexamination of the best reviews and essays.

Guide to the Diplomatic History of the United States. Samuel F. Bemis and Grace G. Griffin. Washington, D.C.: Government Printing Office, 1935. Reprinted, Gloucester, Mass.: Peter Smith, 1959.

This guide is the best source extant for facts on American diplomatic history up to 1921. Part 1 guides one chronologically toward books, journals, chapters of books, manuscript collections, and maps. Part 2 leads one to the best government sources—and explains how to locate them.

International Organization: An Interdisciplinary Bibliography. Michael Haas. Stanford, Calif.: Hoover Institution Press, 1973.

This work has approximately 8,000 entries covering international organizations from the Greek city-states to the present, regional government, proposals for world government, etc.

Nationalism and National Development: An Interdisciplinary Bibliography. Karl W. Deutsch and Richard L. Merritt. Cambridge, Mass.: MIT Press, 1970.

This is an extensive history plus an exhaustive index by author and key word in title.

A Bibliography for the Study of African Politics. Robert B. Shaw and Richard L. Sklar. Los Angeles: African Studies Center, University of California, 1973.

This bibliography contains nearly 4,000 entries from diverse sources.

Urban Environment and Human Behavior: An Annotated Bibliography. Gwen Bell, Edwina Randall, and Judith E. R. Roeder. Stroudsburg, Pa.: Dowden, Hutchinson, & Ross, 1973.

This book is heavily interdisciplinary with extensive annotations. It emphasizes the psychological and sociological aspects of urban life, citizens planning, visual perceptions, aspects of space, etc.

The Vietnam Conflict: Its Geographical Dimensions, Political Traumas, and Military Developments. Milton Leitenberg and Richard Dean Burns. Santa Barbara, Calif.: ABC-Clio, 1973.

This is a brief chronology and a detailed bibliography of the tragic U.S. involvement in Vietnam. The major issues of the war are also delineated.

Book Reviews

Book Review Digest. New York: H. W. Wilson, 1905–.

A monthly publication, this is an indexed reference to selected book reviews drawn from about seventy-five English and American periodicals. With its emphasis on popular rather than scholarly journals, it is arranged by author and has title and subject indexes. Each issue covers from 300 to 400 titles. Excerpts from several reviews are presented for each book, along with a bibliography. For reviews of more scholarly books see *Social Sciences Citation Index* (p. 109) and *Social Sciences Index* (p. 105).

Book Review Index. Detroit: Gale Research, 1965–.

To a great extent, this monthly review with quarterly and annual cumulations supplements the *Book Review Digest.* The index lists current book reviews in the social and natural sciences, although no excerpts of reviews are given, and there is an author index only.

Perspective: Monthly Review of New Books in Government, Politics, and International Affairs. Washington, D.C.: Heldef Publications, 1972–.

Every monthly issue contains approximately twenty concise reviews broken down by the subfields in political science. The reviews are written by specialists in each subfield, and they are signed. Unlike reviews in a general periodical, these reviews emphasize the specialized issues involved in each subfield; i.e., a review of a book on the presidency would emphasize how the book fits into the various political science theories regarding presidential power. Also see *The Political Science Reviewer* (p. 154).

Data and Statistics

GENERAL SOURCES OF DATA
Council of Social Science Data Archives. Ralph L. Bisco, ed. New York: Wiley-Interscience, 1970.

This publication coordinates the projects of nearly every data archive in the nation and in Canada. It distributes to members information on the accessibility of particular survey data in the U.S. and abroad. The CSSDA invites queries from students regarding the location of data in the social sciences.

Directory of Data Bases in the Social and Behavioral Sciences. Vivian S. Sessions, ed. New York: Published in cooperation with the City University of New York by Science Associates International, 1974.

Today most colleges have a computer facility, and many political science professors have an interest in class research projects utilizing computer-based data. For either purpose, this directory is invaluable because it lists hundreds of sources of computer-based data, stating the nature of the data, their form, how they were obtained, and how the researcher can obtain them.

International Guide to Electoral Statistics. Stein Rokkan and Jean Meyriat, eds. The Hague: Morton, 1969.

This is a series of elaborate essays describing how to locate election data in fourteen European countries. It also includes detailed historical material on the electoral process in each country.

SPECIALIZED SOURCES OF DATA

Federal Statistics

American Statistics Index. Washington, D.C.: Congressional Information Service, 1973–.

This index, published annually with monthly supplements, is a master guide to the statistical publications of the U.S. Government. In addition to a comprehensive index by subject, issuing agency, and author, there is an additional index by statistical category. In this latter index you could find, for example, a listing of all current statistics which include breakdowns by race, sex, age, etc. The actual entries contain a concise abstract of each statistical publication.

Directory of Federal Statistics for Local Areas: A Guide to Sources. U.S. Bureau of Census. Washington, D.C.: Government Printing Office, 1966.

One of the most useful federally produced aids in tracking data significant at the state and local levels, this publication is, in a real sense, a source book to federal sources. If a local political or governmental problem is the topic for research, this Bureau of Census directory will give quick access to the most helpful background documents.

Guide to U.S. Government Statistics. 3rd ed. John L. Andriot. Arlington, Va.: Documents Index, 1961–.

This guide indexes federal statistical sources by subject and outlines the statistical output of each agency.

ELECTION DATA

America Votes: A Handbook of Contemporary American Election Statistics. Richard M. Scammon, ed. Pittsburgh, Pa.: University of Pittsburgh Press, 1956–.

This is a prodigious biennial collection of voting statistics; it covers all the national elections from 1954 to the present, state by state. The detailed vote breakdown includes national, state, and county election statistics. State and county figures include total vote–Republican, Democratic, and splinter parties. Each national table is followed by a brief listing of the candidates and their national vote with an identification of the characteristics of the state vote. Special aspects of the electoral college vote are included, and any variations between the plurality figures in these national tables and the Republican-Democratic plurality figures in the state sections are listed. Each state data section is followed by notes giving a detailed composition of the vote and indicating any special circumstances of the state vote–canvassing problems, organization of new counties, dual elector tickets, and so forth.

The major sources for the first volume of this collection are the two pioneer research studies of Edgar Eugene Robinson, *The Presidential Vote, 1896-1932* (Stanford, Calif.: Stanford University Press, 1934), and *They Voted for Roosevelt: The Presidential Vote, 1932-1944* (Stanford, Calif.: Stanford University Press, 1947).

Congressional Roll Call: A Chronology and Analysis of Votes in the House and Senate. Washington, D.C.: Congressional Quarterly Service, 1970–.

For each congressional session, this guide shows the vote lineup, bill by bill, with special subject-matter and topical indexes.

Presidential Ballots, 1836-1892. W. Dean Burnham. Baltimore, Md.: Johns Hopkins Press, 1955.

In addition to exhaustive data, this book includes incisive essays on party politics during the era of sectionalism.

Canada Votes: A Handbook of Federal and Provincial Election Data. Howard A. Scarrow. New Orleans: Hauser Press, 1962.

This handbook contains relatively complete election results for the period covered, in addition to descriptive essays on Canadian politics.

The International Almanac of Electoral History. Thomas J. Mackie and Richard Rose. London: Macmillan, 1974.

Twenty-three western nations have held contested elections since World War II. This source supplies a brief chapter on the political history of each of these countries. These chapters are especially useful for comparative data because of the standard format.

Convention Decision and Voting Records. 2nd ed. Richard C. Bain and Judith H. Parris. Washington, D.C.: Brookings Institution, 1973.

This work analyzes each political convention from 1832 to the present (organization, rules, factions, votes) and then relates convention behavior to the respective formal elections.

1972 Federal Campaign Finances, Interest Groups and Political Parties. Washington, D.C.: Common Cause, 1973.

The raw data of political finance are found in this book: who received how much from whom. There are only a few pages of interpretation but several volumes of facts. These data are extensive enough to correlate with voting records or any other behavioral indicators. A rich source.

Source Books of American Presidential Campaign and Election Statistics, 1948-1968. John H. Runyon, Jennefer Verdini, and Sally S. Runyon. New York: F. Ungar, 1971.

One might think that the data on electing the president would be readily available, but it is seldom compiled in a usable form. The campaign itineraries, for example, are seldom as easily available as in this work. There are also considerable data on media exposure and cost, campaign staffs, voting in preference primaries, etc.

A Statistical History of the American Presidential Elections. Svend Petersen. New York: Ungar, 1963.

This is useful as a compilation. It contains complete statistics on American presidential elections, with tables for each of the fifty states and each of the eleven historical parties.

PUBLIC OPINION AND ATTITUDES

Public Opinion, 1935-1946. Hadley Cantril. Princeton, N.J.: Princeton University Press, 1951.

This is a massive collection of public opinion polls during these years. While dated, the topical range is extensive, and the material could be useful for comparative purposes.

Public Opinion: Changing Attitudes on Contemporary Political and Social Issues. Robert Chandler. New York: R. R. Bowker, 1972.

This contains polls commissioned by CBS News on the important issues of the late 1960s and early 1970s: Women's rights, marijuana, the environment, etc. Results are broken down in terms of an interesting set of categories: parents of reform-oriented youth, parents of radical youth, etc. There is extensive comment and analysis.

The Harris Survey Yearbook of Public Opinion: A Compendium of Current American Attitudes. New York: Louis Harris and Associates, 1971.

The Harris organization polls cover far more areas than are published in newspapers. The breakdown and subdivision of each question are very detailed in this compendium, which contains useful basis data for research.

OPINION POLLS

California Poll. San Francisco: Survey Research Services.

The California electorate is one of the most significant in the nation as a harbinger of future trends. This poll, concentrated within the state, polls Californians on the hottest issue at a particular time and publishes results thirty-five to forty-five times a year.

Gallup Opinion Index. (Formerly *Gallup Political Index*) Princeton, N.J.: Gallup International, 1965–.

Although the Gallup opinion polls are well known and their findings are published regularly in many newspapers, these polls are often neglected by student researchers because of the difficulty of locating a particular poll in an unindexed newspaper. This monthly publication offers an answer to that problem through the publication of monthly surveys covering a wide range of subjects, from the Supreme Court to the "Most Admired Women."

Minnesota Poll. Otto A. Silha, ed. Minneapolis, Minn.: Minneapolis Star and Tribune, 1964–.

This poll is published in the Sunday editions of the *Minneapolis Tribune*; a twenty-year summary was published in 1964 under the title, *Twenty Years of Minnesota Opinion, 1944-1964: Minneapolis Tribune's Minnesota Poll.*

Roper Public Opinion Poll. Williamstown, Mass.: Williams College.

The most exhaustive file of poll data in existence, this source concentrates on all academic and professional poll and survey groups from around the world. The surveys and studies are available to students on cards or tapes at reasonable rates.

The Gallup Poll: Public Opinion, 1935-1971. George H. Gallup. New York: Random House, 1972.

This compilation contains extensive polls on almost every conceivable question and includes comments and interpretations. The results are subdivided along significant lines—age, race, sex.

COMPARATIVE AND RELATIONAL DATA

The Comparative International Almanac. Morris L. Ernst and Judith A. Posner, eds. New York: Macmillan, 1967.

    This work is an excellent source of comparative (as opposed to raw) data about nations. It contains information in the form of rates, ratios, estimates, and comparisons, as well as such particular items as suicide rates, phones-per-1,000-population, life expectancies, and literacy rates. Organization is based on a country-by-country format plus a topical country-by-country ranking.

A Cross Polity Survey. Arthur S. Banks and Robert Textor. Cambridge, Mass.: MIT Press, 1968.

    This survey is a basic source of both data in comparative politics and the methodology for using it. The bulk of the work consists of carefully edited computer printouts in sentence form covering a broad range of social, economic, and political data on every independent nation in the world. The data, along with the contextual explorations, are useful for research on an infinite number of topics.

Social Indicators. Washington, D.C.: Office of Management and Budget and U.S. Department of Commerce, 1973–.

    This irregularly issued publication groups data around major significant goals: good health, long life, fear of crime, etc. The status of the population is then measured against major social indicators. The focus is on the end products (not the institutions delivering the services) and on actual educational attainment rather than on school budgets. Each topic includes a brief essay as well as colorful, concise, easy-to-read charts and graphs. This is clearly a first stop if you are interested in a major problem area.

World Handbook of Political and Social Indicators. 2nd ed. Charles Lewis Taylor and Michael C. Hudson. New Haven, Conn.: Yale University Press, 1972.

Many sources containing statistical data are difficult to relate to topics in political science. With this source, however, one can write an original research paper using basic, politically relevant data. For example, the work contains detailed material on political protest and executive change, foreign aid, telephones per 1,000, riots, ethnic minorities, urbanization, etc. If you want to write an exciting *data-based* paper, this is your best source. Included are essays on interpreting the data, computer programming, and analysis.

DEMOGRAPHIC AND HISTORICAL STATISTICS
Compendium of Social Statistics. New York: United Nations, 1963–.

This yearly compendium contains statistics that show the conditions of life and work in the nations of the world, infant mortality, dwelling size, expenditure levels, labor force, and conditions of employment.

Congressional District Data Book and Congressional District Data Book Supplement: Redistricted States. Washington, D.C.: Government Printing Office, 1961–.

The particular value of this biennial supplement to the *Statistical Abstract of the United States* is that it contains a variety of statistical information that is either unavailable elsewhere or available only piecemeal from a variety of sources. The book organizes this information by congressional district, making it possible to examine congressional voting in terms of the characteristics of each district. It includes items on vital statistics, bank deposits, retail trade, local governments, elections, housing, nonwhite population, and so forth.

County and City Data Book. U.S. Bureau of Census. Washington, D.C.: Government Printing Office, 1952–.

This study has been published annually since 1965; earlier editions covered staggered time periods from 1949 to 1953. It is basically a supplement to the *Statistical Abstract of the United States,* combining two separate earlier publications, *Cities Supplement* (1944) and *County Data Book* (1947). It covers 144 items for each county in the United States and 148 items for each of the 683 cities having 25,000 or more inhabitants. Items for counties include population, dwelling units, retail trade, wholesale trade, selected service trades, manufacturers, vital statistics, and agricultural units. For city units, government, finances, school systems, hospitals, and climate are added. It also contains similar information classified according to such geographic regions and divisions as states and standard metropolitan areas. Descriptive text and source notes are included.

Demographic Yearbook. Statistical Office. New York: United Nations, 1949–.
This book offers detailed world figures on population, projected trends, etc.

Economic Almanac. New York National Industrial Conference Board. New York: Macmillan, 1940-1964.
Although not a comprehensive work, this irregularly published work contains information about business, labor, and government in the more prominent political powers of the world. The statistics for the United States are the most complete. It also contains a general index, a special index on Canada, and a glossary of terms. One can learn, for example, how much the average production worker in Los Angeles earns per hour or how many people will be employed in certain occupations by 1980.

Historical Statistics of the United States, Colonial Times to 1957. U.S. Bureau of Statistics. Washington, D.C.: Government Printing Office, 1960.

This is a supplement to the *Statistical Abstract of the United States,* which contains more than 8,000 statistical studies grouped mostly into yearly periods. It covers economic and social development from 1610 to 1957 and includes definitions of terms and descriptive text. Source notes provide a guide for students who wish to read the original published sources for further reference and data. It contains a complete subject index alphabetically arranged.

Statistical Abstract for Latin America. Center of Latin American Studies. Los Angeles: University of California, 1955–.

This annually issued volume presents current statistical data on all Latin American nations and their dependencies. Information is offered on area, population, social organization, economic characteristics, finances, foreign trade, and other special topics. Notes and source information accompany its tables; it contains an adequate bibliography.

Statistical Abstract of the United States. U.S. Bureau of Census. Washington, D.C.: Government Printing Office, 1879–.

Published annually, this work is a recognized, reliable summary of statistics on the social, political, and economic organization of the United States. It also serves as a guide to other statistical publications and sources through the introductory text to each section, the source notes for each table, and the bibliography of sources. Here one can find information of primarily national concern. Also included, however, are many tables for regions and individual states and statistics for the Commonwealth of Puerto Rico and other outlying areas of the United States.

Additional information for cities, counties, metropolitan areas, congressional districts, and other small units is available in supplements to the abstract (such as *County and City Data Book*; *Congressional District Data Book*; *Historical Statistics of the U.S., Colonial Times to 1957, Continuation to 1962 and Revisions*). The *Statistical Abstract* is the most reliable source for such data as births, deaths, marriages, and divorces; number of physicians, dentists, and nurses; immigration and naturalization; law enforcement, courts, and prisons; geography and climate; public lands and parks; recreation and travel; elections; and incomes.

Statesman's Year Book: Statistical and Historical Annual of the States of the World. London and New York: Macmillan, 1864–.

A great yearbook of more than general value, this book offers a yearly update of economic, political, and social statistics as well as information on international organizations and on every country functioning during the preceding year. The data include each nation's constitution, political and governmental structure, financial basis, gross national product, court system, etc.

United Nations World Economic Survey. (Department of Economic and Social Affairs). New York: United Nations, 1945-1947.

Yearly charts interpret the economic trends of the world in this survey. This book spawns a supplement of detailed studies of entire continental regions.

United Nations Statistical Yearbook. New York: United Nations Statistical Office, 1949–.

This is a continuation of the *Statistical Yearbook of the League of Nations, 1927-1945.* Because of the upheaval of World War II, it was not published between 1945 and 1949. Its tables cover world population, manpower, agriculture, production, mining, construction, consumption, transportation, external trade, wages, prices, national income, finance, social statistics, education, and culture. A ten-to-twenty-year period is generally given for each series of statistics. It is arranged by subject and has a nation index, and it is printed in French and English. Current data for many tables are published regularly by the United Nations Statistical Office in its *Monthly Bulletin of Statistics.*

United Nations Yearbook of National Accounts Statistics. New York: United Nations Statistical Office and Department of Economic and Social Affairs, 1958–.

This work concerns itself with the gross national product of each nation and generally includes a rather complete financial picture (government spending and income, consumer consumption, etc.).

Dictionaries

In "Political Dictionaries: A Bibliographic Essay," (see page 24) Clement Vose noted that political dictionaries differed in several important respects. Most important among his distinctions for the student researcher concerns whether the dictionary contains mainly definitions of politically oriented words or whether it actually is a work on political topics that happens to be arranged in alphabetical order. Both types of dictionaries are useful, depending on the student's need.

First, there is the relatively straightforward political dictionary that emphasizes names, court cases, events, and common political meanings. This type provides ready definitions for the catchwords of the last generation, such as "McCarthyism" or "community action." If your instructor seems always to be making references to people, places, and events that you have never heard of or uses familiar words in unfamiliar ways, this type of dictionary can be helpful.

The following are useful dictionaries in this category:

Dictionary of Political Science. Joseph Dunner, ed. Totowa, N.J.: Littlefield, Adams, 1970.

The American Political Dictionary. Jack C. Plano and Milton Greenberg. 3rd ed. Hinsdale, Ill.: Dryden, 1972.

The International Relations Dictionary. Jack C. Plano and Roy Olton. New York: Holt, Rinehart & Winston, 1969.

Additional reference-type dictionaries of a specialized nature are the following:

Acronyms and Initialisms Dictionary. 4th ed. Ellen Crowley and Robert Thomas, eds. Detroit: Gale Research, 1973, with supplements.

In recent years, rapid changes in technology and world events have given us new ways of identifying already familiar persons (JFK, LBJ, etc.) as well as many new political organizations and slogans that have never been known by anything but their acronyms: COMSAT (Communications Satellite Corporation); GOO (Get Oil Out of Santa Barbara); NOW (The National Organization of Women); OWL (Older Women's Liberation); etc. The nationally prominent and the obscure, the profound and the humorous—this reference guide contains them all.

Black's Law Dictionary: Definition of Terms and Phrases of American and English Jurisprudence, Ancient and Modern. 4th ed. St. Paul, Minn.: West, 1951.

This is the definitive law dictionary. Since legal terms are often part of political controversy, it is helpful to have access to precise definitions of such terms as "indeterminate sentence," "covenant," and "beyond a reasonable doubt."

DICTIONARIES AS IN-DEPTH STUDIES

American Political Terms: An Historical Dictionary. Hans Sperber and Travis Trittschuh. Detroit: Wayne State University Press, 1962.

This differs from the above dictionaries in that it emphasizes the historical derivation of terms. For example, this dictionary shows how the term *silk stocking* as it refers to the wealthy elite, was used by Thomas Jefferson in 1812 and has been used by numerous others since. When using this dictionary, you would probably not be looking up "long hair" because you did not know what the term meant but rather because you would like to know the origin of the term in American politics.

In this instance, the author notes references to long-haired radicals at the time of the Civil War, and then he traces the use of the phrase to the present.

In contrast to simple word definition or even historical derivation, Vose notes that the emphasis in some political dictionaries is on the unity of the work—not just on the individual entries. This is exemplified by prefaces or introductions, essays on the method and sources used, indexes, and cross references. Dictionaries of this type are truly essays on politics that one can simply pick up and read—but also use to enrich almost any piece of research.

The following dictionaries, in varying degrees, fit into that category. Each emphasizes special areas in the study of politics. The most exciting (and easily readable cover to cover) is

The New Language of Politics: An Anecdotal Dictionary of Catchwords, Slogans and Political Usage. William Safire. New York: Collier, 1972.

This dictionary provides the origin of such phrases as "dirty tricks department." The author is a former reporter, practicing politician, and Nixon staffer. A fascinating essay on the origins of political terms precedes the body of the work. Especially interesting in this essay are all the new terms that have emerged since the first printing of the work in 1968.

For example, if your paper is dealing with changing political ideas, campaigns, or programs, a reading of the twelve pages from "new political use of" through "new politics" will enable you to write with a good deal more perception and clarity about political change.

Similar dictionaries in more specialized areas follow:

The Language of Cities: A Glossary of Terms. Charles Abrams. New York: Viking, 1971.

This emphasizes terms in the areas of urban renewal, land use, planning, and community politics. It shows how the forces of history, economics, and government programs have all combined to develop a new "language." For example, if you are concerned with urban political behavior, the entry on urban personality will help explain why urban man behaves as he does.

A Dictionary of Modern War. Edward Luttwak. New York: Harper & Row, 1971.
    This work includes both technical terms such as "bloodhound" (a British missile) and conceptual terms with a precise military meaning such as "threshold" (a demarcation line between particular levels of violence between states).

A Dictionary of Politics. Rev. ed. Walter Laqueur, ed. New York: The Free Press, 1971.
    This dictionary emphasizes factual events from recent history rather than philosophical meanings. For example, in this book one can find the political meaning of "Little Rock, Arkansas," the "Subversive Activities Control Board," the "Kennedy Round" or "Maxim Litinov."

A Dictionary of Political Analysis. Geoffrey Roberts. New York: St. Martin's Press, 1971.
    This emphasizes methodological terms, concepts such as "black box technique," forms of organization, categories, and political ideologies; it mostly excludes concrete references such as court cases, names, places, and events.

A Guide to Communist Jargon. Robert N. C. Hunt. New York: Macmillan, 1957.
    This book consists of in-depth essays that thoroughly explore the meanings of terms as used by Communist (mostly Soviet) writers. "Cosmopolitanism," for example, is considered a reactionary force of international feeling because it urges people to renounce their struggle for national independence. This guide can also be used as a primer on Communist ideology.

Dissertations

Dissertation Abstracts International. Ann Arbor, Mich.: University Microfilms, 1938–.

As a major source on doctoral dissertations in the United States, this publication offers a brief abstract of each paper, with emphasis on the methods and conclusions of the study. Available in both microfilm and full-size editions, it is compiled monthly.

Doctoral Dissertations in Political Science in Universities in the United States. Currently appearing in the fall issue of *P.S.,* the newsletter of the American Political Science Association, Washington, D.C.

Besides including some dissertations not available from University Microfilms, this publication offers a list of dissertations in progress. Although some are never completed, they can be excellent idea material.

Encyclopedias

GENERAL ENCYCLOPEDIAS

Encyclopedia International. New York: Grolier, 1969.

It is difficult to publish a new encyclopedia that can compete in scope and quality with the established sets, but with yearly revisions the *Encyclopedia International* is doing just that. It is a general encyclopedia similar to *Compton's* and *Collier's.* It is especially readable, with unusual headings and subheadings that heighten reader interest; it also includes such helpful and practical information as lists of colleges, study aids, and career guides.

Compton's Pictured Encyclopedia and Fact-Index. Chicago: Encyclopaedia Britannica, 1922–.

Compton's with yearly revisions is a good all-around reference source. Although it does not attempt to provide the depth of the *Britannica* or the *Americana,* it is especially helpful as a first reference source, and the articles are well written and fully keyed to school curricula. There are extensive bibliographies grouped for different educational levels. Each volume has a fact index leading the reader to a large selection of short factual and biographical entries.

Collier's Encyclopedia. New York: Crowell-Collier and Macmillan, 1949–.

This is a strong, clearly written, well-indexed general encyclopedia also revised yearly. It is reliable and often has enough depth for freshmen and sophomore assignments, although it is not exhaustive. It is a good first source with excellent bibliographies and indexes.

The Encyclopedia Americana. New York: Americana Corporation, 1829–.

This is the strongest source for all aspects of American life and culture, including, of course, American politics. Articles are written by leading scholars, with especially strong coverage of recent American history. The bibliography is extensive and so authoritative that it is frequently consulted by librarians. It is revised yearly.

The New Encyclopaedia Britannica. 15th ed. Chicago: Encyclopaedia Britannica, 1974.

The term *new* is certainly appropriate for this encyclopedia. The entire work has been massively reorganized and is, in effect, two encyclopedias plus a one-volume outline of knowledge.

1. The Propedia, one volume, is an outline of knowledge and a guide to the encyclopedia. It is, in effect, a table of contents for the rest of the work with introductory essays on the main areas of knowledge.
2. The Micropedia is a ten-volume ready reference encyclopedia. No article in it is longer than 750 words. It is useful for facts, names, dates, and quick explanations.

3. The Macropedia is intended to contain knowledge in depth. It consists of extensive essays, which one reads for education as well as for information. Some of the essays are excellent, and this source is especially worth investigating if the longer articles are relevant to your topic. For example, the five-page essay on "Political Power" delineates the various applications of the term, the context of power, leadership, power in groups, and community power structures. There is also a good working bibliography that could be developed into many topics for a paper.

ENCYCLOPEDIAS IN THE SOCIAL SCIENCES

International Encyclopedia of the Social Sciences. David L. Stills, ed. 17 vols. New York: Macmillan and The Free Press, 1968.

These volumes constitute an exhaustive updating of the *Encyclopedia of the Social Sciences.* The set contains hundreds of classic articles by the world's leading social scientists, each article defining an entire field of study. The seventeen volumes include a 349-page introduction in two parts: (1) A discussion of the meaning of the social sciences and an outline of their chronological development; and (2) a nation-by-nation survey of the disciplines involved in the social sciences. The main portion of the work deals with the important concepts in political science, economics, law, anthropology, sociology, penology, and social work. About a quarter of the work is composed of biographical sketches. All entries are alphabetically listed with cross references and a subject index.

Encyclopedia of the Social Sciences. E. R. A. Seligman and Alvin Johnson, eds. 15 vols. New York: Macmillan, 1930-1935.

Hundreds of international scholars prepared this comprehensive survey of the fields of social science in the early 1930s. They produced a work that was considered the most important in the field. It is no longer in print, having been superseded by the *International Encyclopedia of the Social Sciences.* However, many of the articles are classics in their field and would still be useful in a paper stressing the development of ideas.

Government Documents

GENERAL GUIDES TO GOVERNMENT DOCUMENTS

Congressional Information Service Index to Publications of the United States Congress. Washington, D.C., 1970–.

Congressional documents contain extensive information on almost every important area of public policy. Without some sort of in-depth index, such as this publication, these reports would be lost to the researcher.

The *CIS Index* analyzes the hundreds of congressional hearing reports and other documents published each year, indexing them by subject so that the researcher can readily identify committee members, witnesses, etc. Moreover, it offers a summary of each document.

Government Publications and Their Use. 2nd rev. ed. Laurence F. Schmeckebier and Roy B. Eastin. Washington, D.C.: Brookings Institution, 1969.

This work describes the basic guides to government publications; indicates the uses and limitations of available indexes, catalogues, and bibliographies; explains the systems of numbering; calls attention to outstanding compilations or series; and advises the student as to the various ways of obtaining the publications. The second edition reflects the many changes—and the growth—in the number of government publications over the last ten years. Referring to the first edition, *Library Journal* remarked: "Nowhere but in Schmeckebier is there such a clear disposition of the quirks involved in the issuing of government documents, and the best ways to work with indexes and keys to this primary research material."

Subject Guide to Major U.S. Government Publications. Ellen Pauline Jackson. Chicago: American Library Assoc., 1968.

Because the official guides index government publications under the name of the issuing agency, which may not be known to the researcher, few students, on starting their inquiries, can identify the important government publications relevant to their topic. This guide gives an annotated bibliography of key government documents on general topics, such as "nuclear disarmament," as well as suggested cross references.

SPECIALIZED GUIDES TO GOVERNMENT DOCUMENTS

International Organizations
United Nations Documents Index (also *The Annual Cumulative Index*). New York: Documents Index Unit, United Nations, 1950–.

The UN documentation system is shockingly cryptographic and would be impossible to penetrate without this key, published monthly. A general description of the documents is to found in *A Guide to the Use of United Nations Documents* (see below). But this index must be used if one is to keep abreast of or locate specific documents. The index is in three parts: Series A, Subjects; Series B, Countries; Series C, List of Documents.

A Guide to the Use of United Nations Documents, Including Reference to the Specialized Agencies and Special UN Bodies. Brenda Brimmer. Dobbs Ferry, N.Y.: Oceana, 1962–.

Another guide-type volume, this publication supplies the researcher with an exhaustive description of the documents classification system, a list of the many UN publications, and various approaches to research projects in general.

State and Local Documents
Index to Current Urban Documents. Westport, Conn.: Greenwood Periodicals, 1972–.

This is the only guide to reports on urban problems issued by the larger cities and counties in the United States and

Canada. For example, if you are interested in manpower training programs, you would find references to reports from major cities. It is useful if you are looking for first-hand resources.

Legislative Research Checklist. Chicago: Council of State Governments, 1947–.

If you are writing on an area of domestic public policy, the chances are that some state legislative agency has published a report on your topic. This publication will help you find it.

Monthly Checklist of State Publications. Washington, D.C.: Government Printing Office, 1910–.

So far no one has been able to list all state publications, but this list of approximately 1,500 such publications per month is a first step in bringing this material together. The documents are arranged by state, and there is an annual index.

State Manuals, Blue Books, and Election Results. Charles Press and Oliver Williams. Berkeley, Calif.: Institute of Governmental Studies, University of California, 1962.

Every state differs in the manner in which it makes public political and governmental information available. This source explains what is available in your state.

U.S. Government Documents

Legally Available U.S. Government Information as a Result of the Public Information Act. Matthew J. Kerbec. Arlington, Va.: Output Systems Corporation, 1970.

This is a ponderous work because it contains each agency's official policies on the release of information. Nevertheless, it can be valuable if you are seeking particular information from the federal government and wish to know your rights before you visit the relevant agency. See the section on "Freedom of Information" on page 166.

Popular Names of U.S. Government Reports: A Catalogue. Donald Wisdom and William P. Kilroy. Washington, D.C.: Government Printing Office, 1970.

While many significant reports are popularly known by the name of one of the responsible officials, such popular names are seldom part of the official title. This guide leads you to the exact citation when all you have to work on is something like "The Kerner Report."

Shepards Acts and Cases by Popular Names—Federal and State. Colorado Springs, Colo.: Shepards Citations, 1968.

Many important laws are cited by popular names (i.e., the Homestead Act), but if you wish to actually read the law you will need to know the proper legal citation. This source answers such questions.

Periodical Indexes

GENERAL PERIODICAL INDEXES
Public Affairs Information Service Bulletin. Robert S. Wilson, ed. New York: Public Affairs Information Service, 1915–.

This index, with annual cumulations, unifies a wide variety of sources concerned with public affairs. Besides periodicals, it lists books, pamphlets, and government documents. The subjects include economics, social conditions, politics, and international relations. Most entries also include brief explanations of the item.

Social Sciences Index. New York: H. W. Wilson, 1916–.

This index, which has quarterly compilations, provides the best source for developing an academic and theoretical focus for a term paper. For example, in referring to general headings such as "interest groups," one will find scholarly articles outlining the pros and cons of the various political science approaches to the study of interest groups. These articles will provide a useful frame of reference for the study of a particular group. In June

1965 the name of this reference was changed from *International Index* to *Social Science and Humanities Index*. More recently a separate *Humanities Index* was published. Book reviews are now indexed separately at the end of each volume.

Also check the *Universal Reference System* (page 78), which includes periodicals.

ADDITIONAL INDEXES

Popular Magazine Indexes
Poole's Index to Periodical Literature. Rev. ed. Gloucester, Mass.: Peter Smith, 1938.

Although not as comprehensive as the *Readers' Guide to Periodical Literature,* this is still the best index of nineteenth-century periodicals. It includes poems and stories and covers approximately 1800-1906. It can be used to research such subjects as the political attitudes expressed in American periodicals of that time.

Readers' Guide to Periodical Literature. New York: H. W. Wilson, 1901—.

This is the major periodical reference source that lists author and subject in a single index and covers the most popular, nontechnical periodicals in the English language.

Newspaper Indexes
Alternative Press Index. Toronto, Canada: Alternative Press Center, 1969—.

A whole host of important current issues are covered quite differently in nontraditional than in traditional newspapers. These include gay liberation, antiwar efforts, alternative life-styles, etc. This source indexes by subject 188 alternative newspapers, lists them by complete name and tells where they can be obtained.

Index to the Christian Science Monitor. Boston: Christian Science Monitor, 1960–.

This index is published monthly with semiannual and annual cumulations.

Index to the Times. John Gurnett, ed. Reading, England: Newspaper Archive Developments, 1906–.

Index: *Chicago Tribune, Los Angeles Times, New Orleans Times-Picayune, Washington Post.* Newspaper Indexing Center. Wooster, Ohio: Bell and Howell, 1972–.

These four important newspapers are indexed separately. Your library may have some or all the indexes.

New York Times Index. New York: New York Times, 1851-1906 and 1912–.

This index is the major reference source for an accurate chronological list of important events. Published semimonthly with annual cumulations since 1930, this publication presents an extensive and detailed look at the world news as reported by the *New York Times.* It cites the date, page, and column, with many cross references, and serves as a reference for material in other newspapers as well. One of the features that students find most attractive is the brief synopsis under each entry, which frequently makes reference to the newspaper itself unnecessary.

The Wall Street Journal Index. New York: M. Dow Jones, 1967–.

Special Purpose Indexes

Biography Index. New York: H. W. Wilson, 1947–.

This quarterly, with cumulations, is the key index to biographical material. It includes all of the biographical references. Entries are arranged alphabetically with a subject index in the back of each issue. This subject index is especially helpful in attempting to identify important individuals in a particular field who are receiving public attention.

Cumulative Index to the Proceedings of the American Political Science Association. Washington, D.C.: American Political Science Association, 1904-1912, 1956-1969. Compiled by Mark Iris. Ann Arbor, Mich.: University Microfilms, 1970.

The American Political Science Association is the main professional organization in the United States for political scientists. This index lists scholarly papers presented at its meetings during the given years. It is useful to illustrate how research in a particular area is progressing.

Education Index. New York: H. W. Wilson, 1929–.

This reference, published monthly except for July and August, with compilations, is a subject index to educational periodicals, yearbooks, and bulletins as well as to the publications of the United States Office of Education from the year 1929. It indexes the answers to such questions as: What is the latest method of educating the mentally handicapped? How much money is being spent by the federal government on education?

Energy Index: A Select Guide to Energy Information Since 1970. New York: Environment Information Center, 1973.

This is a massive collection of information on the energy problem, laws, citations, companies, and energy resources. While much of the work is technical, just glancing through it will suggest many fresh avenues of exploration with regard to this crucial problem.

The Environment Index, 1973. A Guide to the Key Literature of the Year. New York: Environment Information Center, 1973.

This index reviews major developments including a summary of key legislation, important patents, and citations to books and films on the environment. Much of the work is highly technical. Still, the book offers the social science researcher specialized references in a convenient form.

Essay and General Literature Index. New York: H. W. Wilson, 1900–.

This index, published semiannually, with accumulations and supplements, specifically catalogs the contents of books rather than periodicals–which is helpful because often essays and articles appear in a book of collected works without being specifically referred to in the title of the book. This index could help locate, for example, an article on "Woodrow Wilson and Southern Congressmen" that appeared in a book edited by Sidney Fine, titled *Recent America* (New York: Crowell-Collier and Macmillan, 1962).

Index to Legal Periodicals. American Associations of Law Libraries. New York: H. W. Wilson, 1909–.

Law journals interpret the law; they are also an excellent source of public policy articles on such topics as the regulation of business. This index contains data on roughly 300 journals and is published monthly with annual cumulations.

New York Times Obituaries Index 1858-1968. New York: New York Times, 1970.

The obituaries of the *New York Times* are far more thorough than those of most newspapers. They are often the most complete biographical information available. This source helps you find this information.

Social Sciences Citation Index. Philadelphia, Pa.: Institute for Scientific Information, 1973.

This work indexes over 1,000 social science periodicals in three new ways. First, a citation index allows you to trace the application of an idea by showing how and where a particular author is cited within a calendar year. Second, there is a source index that, in addition to containing the usual bibliographic information, lists every citation in a particular article. Third, there is "permuterm," in which every significant word in the title is matched with the author of that article.

SUBJECTS OF INFORMATION

People

BIOGRAPHY AND PERSONALITY SKETCHES

Works in this section may be viewed on four levels. First, there are the serious in-depth studies. In most cases such studies do not occur until after the death of the persons studied, but in some cases, such as the Nader work, *Citizens Look at Congress*, the research is completed while the individuals discussed are still active on the political scene. Second, there are the brief factual sketches such as may be found in a Who's Who. These are useful for quick reference, but their information is largely uncritical because it is supplied by the individuals themselves. Many of these directory-type sources are also useful because their data is grouped and compared. Third, there are the news summaries and the brief interpretive works that fit somewhere between the first two categories. These are often guides to or summaries of current journalistic efforts concerning the subject. They lack the academic depth and objectivity of the historical studies, but they contain more information than a Who's Who paragraph. Fourth, there are monographs, a sample of which is included to illustrate the range of special biographical material. And finally, there are special original source materials related to individual facts, quotations, and speeches.

The student should note that the bridge to virtually all this information is the *Biography Index* cited on page 107.

In-Depth Studies

Dictionary of American Biography. New York: Charles Scribner, 1928, with supplements.

A product of the American Council of Learned Societies, this multivolume work differs from most biographical entities in that its entries are balanced essays written after the death of the subjects—not just a collection of facts. The emphasis in the main volumes is naturally upon nineteenth-century figures. More recent supplements concentrate on figures from the 1930s and 1940s. The essay on Harry Hopkins, for example, explains Hopkins' profound impact on the development of American social welfare and World War II diplomacy and tells how his early experience shaped his ideas.

Citizens Look at Congress, Nader Congress Project. Washington, D.C.: Grossman, 1972-1974.

This multivolume work contains the most detailed information available on individual congressmen. The style is hard-hitting and easy to read. The book brings together an analysis of each congressman's district and his voting record, campaign contributions, and political style. It is current as of August 1972.

Notable American Women 1607-1950. A Biographical Dictionary. Edward T. James, Janet Wilson James, and Paul S. Boyer, eds. Cambridge, Mass.: Belknap Press of Harvard University Press, 1971.

Although written before the current interest in women's identity, this work is important because it identifies many women who have made significant contributions in many fields but have not gained historical recognition. Obviously, only a small percentage of the entries are about political activists.

The McGraw-Hill Encyclopedia of Biography, 12 vols. New York: McGraw-Hill, 1973.

This contains well-written articles about 5,000 significant individuals. The emphasis is upon less well-known Third World figures and leaders. The book is useful in that the articles explain *why* particular figures were chosen for discussion. This work is not as thorough as the previously mentioned sources; still, the articles are in narrative form, go beyond a recitation of facts, and include many illustrations.

Brief Biography and Personality Sketches

Almanac of Current World Leaders. Los Angeles, Calif.: Llewellyn, 1958.

This book contains brief biographies of world leaders currently in the news. Special note is taken of those nations in which leadership has changed since the last publication (which is quarterly). There is a listing by nation of heads of state, cabinet ministers, and their political affiliations. Also included is a chronological listing of events involving changes in governmental and other important posts.

Biographical Directory of United States Executive Branch 1774-1971. Robert Sobel, ed. Westport, Conn.: Greenwood Publications, 1971.

In addition to biographies of over 500 cabinet-level officials from colonial days to the present, this book includes useful comparative tables indicating level of education and college attended, birthplace, etc. One could thus easily find all federal officials who had attended a particular college or had been born in a particular town.

Congress Biographical Directory, 1774-1971. Washington, D.C.: Government Printing Office, 1972.

This contains names and limited biographies of all congressmen for the period covered.

Congressional Directory. Washington, D.C.: Government Printing Office, 1809–.

This directory, which appears with every session of Congress, contains short biographical sketches on all members of the United States Congress, each of whom is given a limited number of free copies to distribute to his constituents. It also lists the membership of each congressional committee and outlines the committee assignments given each member. One may locate herein the name of his congressman, a brief sketch of the legislator's life, and the boundaries of his district. Further, information is furnished concerning each member's vote totals in the last several elections.

The major executives of every government agency are also listed, as are members of the diplomatic corps and members of the press who have accredited seating in the congressional press galleries. A pocket edition of this directory contains a photograph of each member of Congress but omits other information.

Congressional Staff Directory. Charles B. Brownson, ed. Washington, D.C.: Congressional Staff Directory, 1959–.

The staffs of individual congressmen as well as congressional committee staffs have for some time been considered important actors in the political system. Frequently, they are difficult to identify, let alone locate. This source identifies who works for whom and provides basic biographical data on each person.

Directories of Scholars, Professors, Statesmen, and Politicians

Although the idiosyncrasies, political biases, and the like concerning professors are common campus gossip, the following directories will lead the researcher to some facts regarding the person behind the lectern. Beyond the usual vital statistics, these books include information on academic specialties, governmental and political experience, and each professor's publications. *Biographical Directory of The American Political Science Association* (Washington, D.C.: American Political Science Association, 1973) is the key source for political scientists; the *Directory of American Scholars, a biographical directory*, 4 vols. (New York: Jacques Cattell Press, R. R. Bowker, 1974) contains data on the many historians involved in teaching and researching politically related subjects.

International Who's Who. London: Europa Publications and Allen and Unwin, 1935–.

Published annually since 1935, this reference contains from 8,000 to 13,000 short biographical sketches on prominent figures of the world. The *International Who's Who* provides brief but reliable information on the subjects, giving name, title, dates, nationality, education, profession, career, works, and addresses.

International Yearbook and Statesmen's Who's Who. London: Burke's Peerage, 1953–.

This volume combines data on political and economic conditions of the world with an international biographical directory of about 10,000 individuals of world renown: statesmen, diplomats, military leaders, clergy, industrialists, and so forth. The information on various nations, arranged alphabetically, is similar to that in the *Statesman's Yearbook* but with more statistical details.

Taylor's Encyclopedia of Government Officials: Federal and State. John Clements, ed. Dallas, Tex.: Taylor, 1967–.

This encyclopedia is a relatively accurate and continually updated work containing information on every major federal and state governmental body in the United States. From the President to state party chairmen, it includes names, photographs, and frequently home addresses, but little else about the subjects. Changes due to new appointments, elections, redistricting, and other events are available to subscribers, and the entire book is reprinted every two years to include updated material.

Who's Who in America: A Biographical Dictionary of Notable Living Men and Women. Chicago: A. N. Marquis, 1899–.

Subjects of these biographies fall into two groups: those selected because of their special prominence or distinction in certain fields, and those included arbitrarily because of their official position or public standing. Included are not only American citizens but persons of all nationalities who are likely to be of interest to Americans. It is supplemented by *Who Was*

Who in America, for all persons deleted because of death; *The Monthly Supplement,* December 1939 to 1956; the *Supplement to Who's Who,* issued quarterly since 1957; the *Ten-Year Cumulative Index, 1939-1949*; and the *Cumulative Index for 1951-1955.* The major publication is revised and reissued biennially.

Who's Who in American Politics. Paul A. Theis and Edmund L. Henshaw, Jr., eds. New York: R. R. Bowker, 1974.

This work, first published to cover the 1973-74 period, is a biographical directory of 12,500 political leaders in the United States. It is a thorough and authoritative publication that is jointly edited by officials of both major parties. The biographical material was gathered mostly by questionnaires, but the editors note in the introduction that in some cases, when they felt the prominence of the biographee warranted inclusion even though his or her questionnaire was not returned, they gathered the necessary data themselves. Biographical data was culled from various sources, and the biographee was asked to verify a proof copy before it was included in the directory.

Who's Who in Government. 1st ed. 1972-1973. Chicago: A. N. Marquis, 1972.

This publication contains the most complete listing of officials in the federal government as well as selected state and local officials. It provides basic biographical data, but the most useful sections may be the two indexes: one by topics, where the researcher may find the key individuals in all the major government policy areas (such as housing programs, airplane hijacking, etc.), and one by government departments.

BIOGRAPHICAL NEWS SUMMARIES
AND BRIEF INTERPRETATIONS
Biography News. Detroit: Gale Research, bimonthly.

Mervyn Dymally is the Lieutenant Governor of California and the first American Black to achieve this office. The most complete biography of Mr. Dymally appeared in the *Sacra-*

mento Bee, and this information would have been otherwise unavailable nationwide had it not been reprinted in *Biography News.* Each bimonthly edition contains a cumulative index and reprints and feature articles from American news media on personalities of national interest.

Current Biography. New York: H. W. Wilson, 1940–.

    Current Biography supplies unbiased, well-written sketches of contemporary personalities in about forty different professional fields. The emphasis is upon figures in the news. The biographies are based mostly upon current news articles that H. W. Wilson indexes. The book contains photographs of each subject, gives the proper pronunciation of the more difficult names, and lists references to additional material. Each issue contains an accrued-list index of the previous issues. Besides the annual compilation, there are ten-year indexes.

Encyclopedia of American Biography. John A. Garraty, ed. New York: Harper & Row, 1974.

    The first half of each 500 word entry in this book is a factual biographical sketch. The second half is an assessment of the individual's whole career (although many of the subjects are still living) by someone with specialized knowledge on the subject. This is followed by a biographical reference. Interpretations are bound to be controversial, but one may find the volume useful for just that reason. The two-paragraph assessments may provide a good jumping off point for defining a proposition about the subject.

A Minority of Members: Women in the U.S. Congress. Hope Chamberlin. New York: Praeger, 1973.

    Written in narrative chronological form, these biographic essays are interpretative and impressionistic, both describing and categorizing individual congresswomen and the districts from which they have been elected.

New York Times Biographical Editions, Reprints on Biographical Material. New York: Arno Press, 1969–.

A weekly collection of all the biographical material in the *New York Times.* This includes obituaries as well as full-length personality sketches.

Women in the United States Congress 1917-1972. Rudolf Engelbarts. Littleton, Colo.: Libraries Unlimited, 1974.

This contains factual sketches and a short interpretative essay on the accomplishments and political style of American congresswomen. It also has a useful bibliography.

SOURCE MATERIAL ON INDIVIDUALS

Presidents and Vice-Presidents of the United States

The Chief Executive–Inaugural Addresses of the Presidents of the United States, from George Washington to Lyndon B. Johnson. Introduction by Arthur Schlesinger, Jr. Commentary by Fred L. Israel, conceived and ed. by Chelsea House Publishers. New York: Crown, 1965.

The commentaries are especially helpful in that they present the historical context of and major issues behind each speech.

Facts About the Presidents. Joseph Nathan Kane. New York: H. W. Wilson, 1974.

This is a thorough compilation of biographical and historical data including much information not usually assembled, such as number of brothers and sisters, key appointments, important firsts, etc.

Treasury of Presidential Quotations. Caroline Harnsberger. Chicago: Follett, 1964.

Did you know that Thomas Jefferson said, "Indeed I tremble for my country when I reflect that God is just"? This and numerous other presidential quotations are organized under specialized subject headings in this source.

Presidential Papers

Once a president leaves office, his papers become a matter of history and are usually published along with comments and explanations by the compiler. While most items of momentous importance have already been extracted by historians, there remains much original research material for the interested student, for "presidential papers" include personal correspondence and excerpts from diaries, memos, and other communications. For example, *The Public Papers and Addresses of Franklin D. Roosevelt* (New York: Macmillan, 1941) contains the contents of messages to Adolph Hitler along with a press conference in which the President is questioned about the meaning of each message. Such books provide good ground for original research.

The Presidents Speak: The Inaugural Addresses of the American Presidents, from Washington to Nixon. 3rd ed. Annotated by Davis Newton Lott. New York: Holt, Rinehart & Winston, 1969.

The annotations are especially helpful in that they highlight key ideas and comparisons to other Presidents.

U.S. Presidents, The State of the Union Messages of the Presidents, 1790-1966. Fred L. Israel, ed. 3 vols. New York: Chelsea House, 1966.

An introductory essay by Arthur Schlesinger, Jr., suggests themes and points upon which to compare various Presidents. The subject index can be very useful.

MONOGRAPHS

American Assassins. Jo Anne Ray. Minneapolis, Minn.: Lerner, 1973.

America has had more than its share of political assassins. Unfortunately, assassins are significant political actors on the American scene. This work contains biographies of significant assassins and would-be assassins from John Wilkes Booth to Sirhan Sirhan.

The New Frontiersmen—Profiles of the Men Around Kennedy. The *Evening Star*. Washington, D.C.: Public Affairs Press, 1961.

The Kennedy generation continues to play an important part on the national scene. Here are sketches of the New Frontiersmen.

Madmen and Geniuses: The Vice-Presidents of the United States. Sol Barzman. Chicago: Follett, 1974.

One-third of our presidents have been vice-presidents. Each of them is described in terms of his background and later career in office.

QUOTATIONS

What They Said in _____. Beverly Hills, Calif.: Monitor, 1969–.

In this work, current lively and interesting quotes by public figures are arranged according to topics. Thus, one can look up what George McGovern, Ronald Reagan, and a host of others have said about "Asia and the Pacific" or look up individual figures such as Gerald Ford to see what he recently said on a particular topic.

Familiar Quotations. John Bartlett, ed. Boston: Little, Brown, 1968.

This is a useful collection of thousands of quotations that have become part of the English language. Bartlett lists each quotation under its author and reprints it within the context of the poem, passage, or article in which it originally appeared. The authors are listed chronologically, and there is a topical index referring to page and author. For instance, the source of the line, "What this country needs is a good five-cent cigar," can be found under *cigar* in the line index. (The source of this quotation, incidentally, is Thomas R. Marshall, Vice-President under Woodrow Wilson.)

Events

WHAT HAPPENED IN HISTORY
An Encyclopedia of World History: Ancient, Medieval, and Modern, Chronologically Arranged. Rev. ed. William L. Langer, ed. Boston: Houghton Mifflin, 1972.

In no other volume can one locate the essential facts of world history so quickly. Using an expanded outline form with important names and dates in boldface type, this single volume covers the recorded history of the world. Extensively indexed, it allows one to expend a minimum of effort to find such data as the chronology of the short Soviet-Finno war of 1939-1940 or the Moslem conquest of Spain in 711-1031.

Historical Atlas. 9th ed. William Robert Shepherd. New York: Barnes & Noble, 1964.

This is a superb one-volume atlas covering the world from about 1945 B.C. to the present. Each map is arranged chronologically (there is no accompanying text). The volume contains an exhaustive index of place names, including classical and medieval Latin place names, many of which do not appear on the maps. These are cross-referenced to the modern forms of the names.

Who Said What (and When and Where and How) in 1971, Vol. 1: Jan.-June. Barbara Bennett and Linda Amster. New York: Quadrangle, 1972.

This source is really based on who said what in the *New York Times.* Quotations are arranged by subject with reference to the *Times* edition in which it appeared. There is an extensive index. It is useful for tracking down fugitive quotations.

WHAT HAPPENED LAST YEAR
The Annual Register of World Events. London: Longmans, 1761–.

This is a British publication first edited by Edmund Burke and heavily emphasizing Great Britain and the Commonwealth in what is considered to be one of the best summaries of year-by-year events. It also covers such areas as political, economic, and cultural events and speeches from around the world, with summaries. The events—political and nonpolitical—are written in notable prose and are integrated into quarterly reports.

Historic Documents of_____. Washington, D.C.: Congressional Quarterly, 1972–.

This brings together the important speeches, documents, and pronouncements from a particular year. It is especially useful to show how quickly the significance of various items can change (see, for example, Richard Nixon's comments on Watergate and the Democratic party platform on energy).

New International Year Book: A Compendium of the World's Affairs. New York: Funk & Wagnalls, 1932–.

This reference work charts the events and progress of the year, classifying each under such categories as politics, foreign affairs, labor, sports, and so on. It is indexed and includes photographs, charts, and detailed statistics.

Survey of International Affairs. London: Oxford University Press for the Royal Institute of International Affairs, 1920–.

This sums up a year in terms of major international events, i.e., 1962 was the year of the Soviet offensive against the United States in Cuba. The Europe Essays are heavily interpretive (see "The Defeat of the Grand Design of U.S., Britain, and France," "The Crisis in the United Nations").

World Almanac and Book of Facts. New York: Newspaper Enterprise Association, 1868–.

Published yearly, first by the *New York World-Telegram and Sun,* the *World Almanac* supplies a wealth of information in every area likely to be investigated. A random sample of the broad spectrum of work includes the latest sports records; Nobel Peace recipients; listings of colleges and universities;

heads of states; brief descriptions of foreign countries; a list of United States art galleries; biographies of Presidents and their wives, cabinet members, Supreme Court judges, and ambassadors; and an explanation of how to make out a will properly.

In the same category as the *World Almanac* and furnishing basically the same information are *Information Please Almanac* (New York: Simon & Schuster, 1944–); *Reader's Digest Almanac,* edited by *Reader's Digest* editors (New York: Funk & Wagnalls, 1966–); and *The Official Associated Press Almanac* (Maplewood, N.J.: Hammond, 1973–).

Yearbook of World Affairs. London Institute of World Affairs. London: Stevens and Sons, 1947–.

This book contains essays of about twenty pages each on current world developments written by recognized scholars. It is a good source for relatively instant scholarship and insight on important world matters. For example, in 1972 it contained "U Thant and His Critics" by Alan James.

Watergate: Chronology of a Crisis. Washington, D.C.: Congressional Quarterly, 1972.

For most researchers, this will provide all the data necessary about Watergate: the events, the people, the consequences. It is done in concise, well-written form and is indexed.

Yearbook on International Communist Affairs. Milorad M. Drachkovitch. Stanford, Calif.: Hoover Institute, 1967–.

This yearbook contains articles on each country of the world by specialists on communist activity for that year.

Yearbook on Human Rights. New York: United Nations Department of Social Affairs, 1947–.

This describes constitutional, legislative, and legal developments in ninety-two states and trust territories—all bearing on human rights.

Yearbook of the United Nations. New York: United Nations Department of Public Information, 1947–.

These annual editions constitute a year-by-year record of the activities of the United Nations. Each edition is designed to present, in a single, fully indexed volume, a compact authoritative account of the deliberations and actions of the United Nations as well as the activities of the intergovernmental agencies related to it.

WHAT HAPPENED LAST WEEK

General Events

Deadline Data on World Affairs. Greenwich, Conn.: Deadline Data, 1956–.

Published four times a month on 5″ × 8″ file cards, the data are arranged alphabetically by country and subfiled under "general," "domestic," or "foreign policy" categories. Occasionally, something is filed by subject, such as "selective service." Since 1968 a monthly compilation of this data has been published under the title *On Record.* This is an especially useful source for a quick summary or chronology of a recent political event.

Facts on File: Weekly World News Digest with Cumulative Index. New York: Facts on File, Inc., 1940–.

This publication records the events of each week in a given year in an unbiased and concise style. Each news item is filed and reported under a specific heading such as world affairs, national affairs, sports, and the like. Each also includes a reference to any previous article on the same topic. However, sources are not listed. There are cumulative monthly, semiannual, and yearly indexes.

Keesing's Contemporary Archives: Weekly Indexed Diary of World Events. H. C. Tobin, and R. S. Fraser Keynsham, eds. Bristol, Eng.: Keesing's, 1931–.

These volumes are mainly a wrapup of news reports for each week, but they also include recent speeches and government documents, prominent obituaries, etc. This service covers world events but is strongest for the United Kingdom and Europe. It is indexed cumulatively into capsules of two weeks, three months, a year, and two years.

News Dictionary. New York: Facts on File, 1974–

This is an unusual source. One simply looks up the topic to find out what happened in that area during the past year. For example, "Hijackings" provides a concise summary of all hijackings by country for the year.

Events in Specific Places
African Recorder. New Delhi: Recorder Press, 1902–.

This publication summarizes events and quotes in African affairs twice monthly from major worldwide newspapers.

Africa Diary. New Delhi: Africa Publications, 1961–.

This is a weekly diary of African events with an index. Although the summaries are brief, they are probably more extensive than you would find in a United States paper. This book provides a good way to follow an event without endless thumbing through newspapers. Sources for each entry are listed. There are quarterly and annual cumulations.

Arab Report and Record. London: Arab Report and Record, 1966–.

Published twice monthly, this work has the usual news summaries plus related statistics such as weekly Arab oil production figures.

Asian Recorder. New Delhi: Asian Recorder, 1955–.

This is a weekly digest of outstanding Asian events with an

index. It summarizes American, European, and Asian news dispatches. It is a ready source of information.

Canadian News Facts: The Indexed Digest of Canadian Current Events. Barrie Martland and Stephen D. Pepper, eds. Toronto, Ont.: Marpep, 1967—.

This digest is a twice-monthly publication that does in-depth wrapups on general news developments in the provincial capitals. It also covers foreign relations.

Latin American Research Review: A Journal for the Communication of Research Among Individuals and Institutions Concerned with Studies in Latin America. Editorial Office. Austin, Tex.: University of Texas, 1965—.

The basic guide to research in Latin American studies, this book usually is divided into parts: "Topic Reviews," four or more pieces outlining research on subjects from literature to taxes; "Reports," which follows the latest trends in research and sources; "Current Research Inventory"—the soul of the entire journal—which lists by university and subject all post-doctoral research reported; "Forum," a discussion of current questions in the area. The journal has been called "an absolute must for any library where there is the slightest interest in Latin American affairs." We agree.

Middle East Record. Daniel Dashon, ed. New York: John Wiley, 1960—.

The Middle East continues to be an important area in world affairs, and often accounts of a particular event there differ. This source presents concise summaries of daily happenings from over 200 newspapers, periodicals, and official reports. When the Palestinian refugees and the Israelis exchange violence, one hears many versions of the incident. This source, with irregular publication, allows the researcher the single best opportunity to draw his own conclusion.

Entities, Groups, Organizations, and Nations

INTERNATIONAL ORGANIZATIONS

A Chronology and Fact Book of the United Nations 1941-1964. Waldo Chamberlain and Thomas Hovet. Dobbs Ferry, N.Y.: Oceana, 1964.

This is a chronological listing of the important acts, events, meetings, membership, etc., of the UN, frequently with brief identifying statements.

European Institutions: Co-operation, Integration, Unification. 3rd ed. Arthur H. Robertson. New York: Matthew Bender, 1973.

This is a complete guide to the many organizations now involved in European integration. It includes political, economic, and social organizations. The essays are both factual and interpretative.

Everyman's United Nations. 8th ed. New York: United Nations Department of Public Information, 1968.

This is the primary source for the structure, functions, and work of the United Nations and its related agencies. A frequently revised handbook, it is broken into four parts. Part I discusses the organization of the United Nations; Part II is concerned with political, social, economic, and security questions; Part III deals with specialized agencies, such as the Food and Agriculture Organization (FAO), the United Nations Educational, Scientific, and Cultural Organization (UNESCO), and many others; Part IV contains an index, the chronology, and a list of the United Nations Information Centers.

Yearbook of International Organizations. Eyvind S. Tew, ed. Brussels, Belgium: Union of International Associations, 1948–.

Of the more than two thousand international organizations listed herein, less than fifty are affiliated with the United Nations—a fact that gives many a young scholar pause. Of course, those not carrying UN credentials do not often make the front pages, but in their particular areas, they are quite influential; without a guide of this type, they would undoubtedly elude most students. Those organizations not carrying UN credentials include a range from the highly political International Peace Association to the relatively esoteric International Association of Art Critics. Each entry covers the general history and a description of the organization and—more important—a direction to sources of further information.

NATIONS OF THE WORLD

The Almanac of World Military Power. Col. T. N. Dupuy, ret., Col. Wendell Blanchard, ret., and Lt. Grace P. Hayes. Dunn Loring, Va.: T. N. Dupuy Associates, 1970.

This biennial work discusses the resources of nations as seen through military eyes. The authors consider all aspects of national power, location, economic power, etc. as aspects of potential military power. Though most of this material is taken from public records, it is nowhere else assembled in this fashion. When a struggle breaks out somewhere on the globe, this source will give you a ready assessment of each nation's potential strength.

China: A Handbook. Yuan-li Wu, ed. New York: Praeger, 1973.

With the renewal of Western contact with Mainland China, this volume of reference essays should be used by an increasing number of students. The essays are all by Western scholars, many of whom are of Chinese origin, however. They are detailed and scholarly, yet readable. Examples: "Sino-Soviet Relations," "Chinese Health and Medicine."

The Europa Yearbook. London: Europa, 1959–.

This yearbook is a comprehensive multi-volume collection of information about all the countries of the world, not just Europe. In addition, this work deals in great detail with international organizations. There is information on daily newspapers, radio and television stations, banking structure, religions, and institutions—all by specific name.

McGraw-Hill Encyclopedia of Russia and the Soviet Union. Michael T. Florinsky, ed. New York: McGraw-Hill, 1961.

Emphasizing events after 1918, this book contains detailed information on people and places, such as the Georgian Soviet Socialist Republic, not found elsewhere.

Political Handbook and Atlas of the World: Parliaments, Parties and Presidents. New York: Council on Foreign Relations, 1927—.

This paperback contains an alphabetical listing of the factual background (heavily political) of all the independent nations of the world and is supplemented with a section of detailed maps. It includes such data as a nation's political structure, its major news media, its land area, its population, and an outline of its political history. Since 1971 it has been updated by a publication entitled *The World This Year.*

Worldmark Encyclopedia of Nations. New York: Harper & Row, 1971.

This five-volume work presents geographic, social, historical, and political facts concerning the various nations of the world in an easy-to-use form. There are large standard subheadings, so one can, for instance, compare the transportation systems in Nigeria and Morocco quickly and easily.

REGIONS AND CONTINENTS

African Encyclopedia. London: Oxford University Press, 1974.

This is a good one-volume source on Africa. In addition to listing a number of African topics not available elsewhere, it provides a detailed index of African subjects and indicates how to deal with them.

Africa: A Handbook to the Continent. Rev. ed. Colin Legum, ed. New York: Praeger, 1966.

This deals with individual African countries, the continent as a whole, and other countries' attitudes toward Africa.

Encyclopedia of Latin America. Helen Delpar. New York: McGraw-Hill, 1974.

This is a specialized source emphasizing the postcolonial or national period of Latin America. The topics themselves provide a good source of ideas for a paper, e.g., the history of women's political rights in Latin America.

UNITED STATES, NATIONAL GOVERNMENTS, AND SUBUNITS

The Almanac of American Politics. Michael Barone, Grant Ujifusa, and Douglas Matthews. Boston: Gambit, 1972–.

This biennial publication is the single best source on congressional districts and members of Congress. Much more than a statistical compilation, it provides a political analysis of each congressional district as well as data on key votes, group meetings of legislators, the census, federal spending, etc.

Congressional Districts in the 1970s. Washington, D.C.: Congressional Quarterly, 1970.

Here are concise summaries of the 435 congressional districts as well as military, industrial, and communications facilities–plus a special section on the impact of the 1972 reapportionment.

Guide to the Congress of the United States: Origins, History, and Procedure. Washington, D.C.: Congressional Quarterly, 1971.

This volume is an in-depth study of Congress; it is essentially factual and politically oriented. It deals both with rules and procedures and how the various factions have used them. It is the definitive factual source on Congress.

Administrative Agencies of the U.S.A. Their Decisions and Authority. Dalmas H. Nelson. Detroit: Wayne State University Press, 1964.

Few works exist in political science on the vast area of administrative law, but administrative orders are very important in political life. This work describes censorship, cease and desist, workmen's compensation, and other administrative rulings.

Encyclopedia of Government Advisory Agencies. Linda E. Sullivan and Anthony T. Kruzas, eds. Detroit: Gale, 1973.

Political scientists have long been interested in the unique role of advisory agencies. Do they control the agencies they advise? Are they a vehicle for special interests? This work lists numerous interagency and related boards, committees, etc., and their members, origins, and affiliations.

American Agencies Interested in International Affairs. Ronald Wasson, ed. The Council on Foreign Relations. 5th ed. New York: Praeger, 1964–.

This guide to several hundred organizations based in the United States covers their purpose and their organizational structure.

United States Government Manual. Washington, D.C.: Government Printing Office, 1935–.

This is the official organization manual of the United States Government. It describes the purpose and programs of most government agencies and lists top personnel. It is the first basic source for information on the federal bureaucracy.

Where Is the CIA. (In English). Dr. Julius Mader. Panorama DDR, Auslangspressedienst GMBH, DDR-1054, Berlin: Wilhelm Pieck Strasse-49, 1970.

Although your library is unlikely to have this East German document, it can be obtained from the above address. It claims to be a documentation of organizations and institutions throughout the world set up by the CIA.

STATE AND LOCAL GOVERNMENTS

Book of the States. Chicago: Council of State Governments, 1935–.

This biennial work is a rich source of authoritative information on the actual structure, working methods, functioning, and financing of state governments. The legislative, executive, and judicial branches are outlined in depth according to their intergovernmental relations and the major areas of public service performed by each. A directory supplement is published in odd-numbered years.

Important statistics are also contained in these volumes: salaries and compensations of state legislators, divorce laws, voting laws and regulations, state departments, welfare budgets and payments, and educational salaries and budgets.

Metropolitan Area Annual. Albany, N.Y.: State University at Albany, Graduate School of Public Affairs, 1966–.

Published annually, this work contains the latest developments in municipal government, various city statistics, directories of municipal officials, directories of state agencies functioning at the local level, and facts on metropolitan area planning commissions. The articles summarize developments in a given year.

Municipal Yearbook. Chicago: International City Management Association, 1934–.

This annual reference work is certainly the best source in its field. It is an authoritative resumé of activities and statistical data of American cities, with emphasis on individual city programs. Attention is devoted to developments in urban counties and metropolitan areas. It contains thorough bibliographies and comprehensive directories of officials.

The National Directory of State Agencies. Matthew J. Vellucci, Nancy D. Wright, and Gene P. Allen. Washington, D.C.: Information Resources, 1974.

This is a national listing of state agencies according to sixty-six categories. It also includes associations of state officials. For example, it lists each state agency and official dealing with government support of the arts.

INTEREST GROUPS AND POLITICAL PARTIES

Encyclopedia of Associations. Detroit: Gale Research, 1975.

Alexis De Tocqueville gave Americans an early clue about our tendency to form associations of all kinds, "religious, moral, serious, futile, restricted, enormous or diminutive." This three-volume work is evidence that the tendency is still operating. Associations are broken down by type, with a geographic and executive index. Each entry includes purpose, activities, and publications. A section on public affairs organizations is of particular interest.

American Jewish Year Book. Morris Fine, Milton Minnelfarb, and Martha Jelenko, eds. New York: American Jewish Committee, 1899/1900–.

American Jews have become an especially active and influential group in American politics with the emergence of the Israeli conflict. This detailed book of essays deals with a wide spectrum of Jewish life in the United States and the world, covering civic, political, and communal issues.

First National Directory of "Rightist" Groups: Publications and Some Individuals. 6th ed. Los Angeles: Alert Americans Association, 1968.

The Who's Who of the political right from the National Fluoridation News to four Reagan for President centers. This book is, however, only a directory of names and addresses and contains no description of entries.

History of U.S. Political Parties. Arthur M. Schlesinger, Jr., gen. ed. 4 vols. New York: Chelsea House, 1973.

A massive one-stop source for a term paper on U.S. political parties, major and minor. After an introductory essay on each party, there are additional essays on the major sources in the field. For example, after an essay on the American Independent Party, this source reprints the party's 1968 platform, a press interview with George Wallace, and Governor Wallace's 1968 Madison Square Garden speech.

Key Influences in the American Right. Ferdinand V. Solara. Denver, Colo.: Polifax, 1972.

In addition to a brief description, one finds in this volume the addresses, officers, membership, etc., of American rightist groups. This source contains an introductory essay and typology of rightist groups and ideas, which can serve as a useful framework for a paper.

Marxism, Communism, and Western Society: A Comparative Encyclopedia. C. D. Kernig, ed. New York: Herder and Herder, 1972.

This book emphasizes individual articles showing that differences exist between East and West. One can see the political meaning of topics usually considered nonpolitical—for example, the Soviet view toward art or the Soviet view of the Western policy of anticommunism.

National Trade and Professional Associations in the United States. Craig Colgate, Jr., ed. Washington, D.C.: Columbia, 1966–.

If anyone had doubts about the importance of business groups in American politics, the experience of Watergate has certainly dispelled that belief. Here are all the players in the game of influencing public policy. Most helpful are key words under which are listed all groups involved in particular areas as well as indexes of budgets from $10,000 (the Socket Screw Products Bureau) to over $1,000,000 (Asphalt Institute) and of key executives.

National Party Platforms 1840-1964 (with a supplement for the 1968 platforms published in 1969). 3rd ed. Kirk H. Porter and Donald Johnson. Urbana, Ill.: University of Illinois Press, 1966.

Even though a political party platform is not often adhered to once the elections are over, it must be considered as an indicator of the goals and internal dissensions of the party. Included are the platforms of many minor parties, as well as those of the two major parties. This work included, for example, the 1960 platforms of the Democratic, Republican, Prohibition Socialist, Socialist, Labor, and Socialist Worker parties.

The Washington Lobby. Washington, D.C.: Congressional Quarterly, 1974.

This summarizes developments in the lobbying over the past five years, touching on law changes, problems of key lobbyists, and lobbying organizations.

World Strength of Communist Party Organizations. Department of State, Bureau of Intelligence and Research. Washington, D.C.: Government Printing Office, 1950.

Here are detailed reports in a readable style of Communist activity in many countries. The reports describe the source of Communist strength, elected officials, election results, etc.

World Communism: A Handbook 1918-1965. Witold S. Sworakowski, ed. Stanford, Calif.: Hoover Institution Press, 1973.

The Communist party has been active in 116 countries during this period. This source contains a brief essay on its activities in each of those countries. The book is a good first source for a variety of topics focusing on the history, organization, techniques of party operation, etc.

FOREIGN RELATIONS

American Foreign Policy: Current Documents. Historical Office of the Bureau of Public Affairs. Washington, D.C.: Government Printing Office, 1941–.

This is a yearly publication that gathers the more

important messages, declarations, treaties, etc. that have surfaced during the year.

Foreign Relations of the U.S.: Diplomatic Papers. Department of State. Washington, D.C.: Government Printing Office, 1862–.

This is the official record of U.S. foreign policy; it contains all documents, papers, and communiques available to the public. It is surprisingly rich in detail and even includes personal correspondence, such as a memorandum of a conversation between U.S. Secretary of State George Marshall and Generalissimo Joseph Stalin. A chance to view history firsthand.

Foreign Relations of the United States: Diplomatic Papers. Washington, D.C.: Government Printing Office, 1861–.

This is a Department of State series that offers the most complete State Department records of the past. Published annually, these books contain a selection of public documents, diplomatic correspondence, messages between the United States and other governments, and departmental memoranda. The content is limited by omission for confidentiality and security as well as an approximately twenty-five year lag in publication.

United States in World Affairs. The Council on Foreign Relations. New York: Harper & Row, 1931-1967. Simon and Schuster, 1968–.

Published yearly, this book is a series of interpretive essays that try to explain American foreign policy. A detailed chronology in the appendix makes this series most useful as an integrator of events. For example, the table of contents for 1966 lists: "What Price a Free Vietnam"; "Origins of the Problem's Two Views"; "End of the Pause"; "Honolulu and After"; "The Debate Continues and So Does the War."

United States Treaties and Other International Acts. U.S. Department of State. Washington, D.C.: Government Printing Office, 1950–.

This is a series of publications listing all treaties and agreements to which the United States has become a party during a given year.

Law, Policies, and Programs

INTERNATIONAL LAW

Constitutions of Nations. Amos J. Peaslee. 4 vols. The Hague: Martians Nijhoff, 1965.

This contains English translations of virtually every national constitution, many of which are far more specific than the U.S. Constitution.

Synopsis of United Nations Cases in the Field of Peace and Security 1946-67. Catherine Teg. New York: Taplinger, 1968.

This is a short work that presents one-page summaries of each action. In an area in which many documents are extremely lengthy, this is a valuable compilation. It is arranged by nation with an appendix on international conflict.

World Treaty Index. Peter Rohn, ed. 5 vols. Santa Barbara: ABC-Clio, 1974.

This index can serve as far more than a simple locater of treaties. It applies the techniques of modern quantitative research to the ancient field of international law. This source can be used as a basis for original research. The multitude of treaties signed by nations of the world have been content analyzed and indexed in depth. For example, if you wish to compare how nations protect their citizens when abroad you could look up "protection of nationals" and find citations to 17 specific treaties dealing with this problem.

NATIONAL LAW

The Constitution and What It Means Today. Edward Samuel Corwin. Revised by Harold W. Chase and Craig R. Dacat. Princeton, N.J.: Princeton University Press, 1973.

This is a definitive work on the United States Constitution. Article by article, amendment by amendment, this authoritative work summarizes the leading legal cases that have shaped the interpretation of the Constitution. For example, if one wishes to know exactly what is meant by the "right to a speedy and public trial," he or she can find in this book a concise summary of applicable cases.

U.S. Senate Factual Campaign Information. Washington, D.C.: Government Printing Office, 1972.

Originally for use by senators in their own reelection campaigns, this is a compilation of state primary laws, previous votes, and relevant administrative and Senate rulings.

The Rights We Have: A Handbook of Civil Liberties. Osmond K. Fraenkel. New York: Crowell, 1971.

The meaning of such terms as "freedom of the press" is constantly changing not only through judicial opinions, but through technology, administrative decisions, and changing mores. This book explains the complex meaning of these terms in clear, concise words. For example, it discusses the question of when the right to express oneself runs into the sanction against disorderly conduct.

U.S. Senate Nomination and Election of the President and Vice-President of the U.S. Including the Manner of Selecting Delegates to National Political Conventions. Washington, D.C.: Government Printing Office, 1972.

Presidential selection is a complex process involving primaries, state conventions, state party rules, and a multitude of laws, national and state. This is the most usable compilation of this data; it is revised frequently.

Index Digest of State Constitutions. 2nd ed. Legislative Drafting Service Research Fund. New York: Columbia University, 1959.

In addition to reprinting the fifty state constitutions with current supplements, this digest allows one to compare how each state deals with a particular problem—such as impeachment.

UNITED STATES POLICIES AND PROGRAMS
The Encyclopedia of U.S. Government Benefits. Roy A. Grisham, Jr. and Paul D. McConaughy, eds. Union City, N.J.: W. H. Wise, 1966.

This reference book lists, describes, and discusses all services and benefits provided by the United States government. It provides answers to the complex question of the citizen's relationship to big government. This is the first book to catalog and detail eligibility for all government services. It is also unique in that it alphabetizes primarily by benefit classification rather than by agency, department, or initiating legislative act. It is both a practical reference and a useful index to the scope and depth of federal programs.

A Guide to Federal Consumer Services. The President's Committee on Consumer Interests. Washington, D.C.: Government Printing Office, 1967.

Over fifty government agencies provide services to the consumer. This guide outlines major purpose and function, legal background of each program, how the law is enforced, and how one contacts the appropriate agency to get help.

Setting National Priorities, the Budget. Washington, D.C.: The Brookings Institution, 1971–.

The federal budget is the major blueprint for government policy, yet it is extremely confusing to the layman. This yearly guide analyzes the budget issue by issue. The chapter on defense, for example, identifies and explains the issues in defense spending—pay, manpower, type of weapons, military forces in Europe, etc. This work is an excellent first source.

The New York Times Guide to Federal Aid for Cities and Towns. Howard S. Rowland. New York: Quadrangle, 1971.

This guide tells "all you ever wanted to know about grants-in-aid but were afraid to ask." Starting with a description of the impact of federal grants on one city, Peekskill, New York, the study then describes how to write an aid proposal and provides an in-depth look at the vast range of federal programs. The programs themselves are arranged in topical sections, with an introductory explanation of federal grants. The source is most likely intended for cities seeking grants.

MAKERS OF LAWS AND POLICIES

Basic Legislative Documents

You can use the basic documents of Congress as primary data sources, provided you have some background on the issue you are studying (which can be gained from the *Congressional Quarterly Weekly Report*) and you are not smothered by the massive output of legislative documents. In the following pages, we shall describe the *basic* legislative documents necessary for a term paper. Most are available in a government depository library, of which there are over a thousand throughout the United States. Some, such as the *Congressional Record,* are available in almost any college library. A few, such as current bills, can be obtained from any congressman. In this instance, be sure to allow enough time (at least ten days) to receive the bills. The basic documents described herein are the following:

1. *Congressional Record*
2. House and Senate journals
3. House, Senate, and conference reports
4. Proceedings of hearings
5. Bills and the digest of public bills
6. *Calendars of the United States House of Representatives and History of Legislation*
7. *Congressional Serial Set*

Note the bibliographic citations on pages 64-65 for the correct way to cite or request a bill or hearing report.

Congressional Record. Washington, D.C.: Government Printing Office, 1873–.

The *Record* is a nearly verbatim account of everything uttered aloud on the floor of Congress as well as of some material not actually spoken but entered as an "extension of remarks." It is published Monday through Friday as long as Congress is in session. The *Congressional Record* is a valuable source because legislators frequently insert letters and articles that are in themselves primary sources of information on topics under discussion.

Prior to 1873 the *Congressional Record* was titled *Congressional Globe* (1833-1873); before that it was called *The Register of Debates* (1824-1837); and even earlier, *Annals of Congress* (1789-1824). It is cataloged under these titles in libraries. Each set consists of fifteen to twenty parts a year, including a separate index. In 1947 the *Daily Digest* volumes were added, which review highlights, list scheduled hearings of Congress, and summarize day-to-day committee activity.

The *Congressional Record* contains a two-part index, consisting of an alphabetical listing of subjects and names and a history of bills and resolutions arranged by their numbers. This second section is thought to be the best available source for tracing the route of a particular bill. Because this is a daily record, the best method of locating information is first to establish the date on which the debate took place.

A student may request to be placed on the mailing list for the *Congressional Record.* It is a free service rendered by legislators to their constituents. However, unless the student is willing to read and digest some 200 pages a day, this would be wasteful, as each legislator is limited to sixty-eight such free subscriptions.

House and Senate journals.

These two separate documents are published by each house at the end of a session. They are essentially official, trimmed-down versions of the *Congressional Record,* with debates and all other matters excluded. Included are motions, votes, and actions taken.

House, Senate, and Conference reports.

These are the reports of the committees dealing with a particular measure. They include data on the actual suggested legislation to be sent to the floor and the majority, minority, and concurring reports—which usually outline the issues around the measure. Especially interesting are reports from conferences, which involve both House and Senate members. When read with an understanding of the context of a measure, which you can gain from the *Congressional Quarterly*, these reports can form the backbone of an original research paper.

Proceedings of hearings.

Congressional hearings are an incredibly rich source of material, but that material must be used intelligently. Appropriations hearings are particularly good. For the results of digging through the proceedings of such hearings, see Aaron Wildavsky, *The Politics of the Budgetary Process* (Boston: Little, Brown, 1973).

The bulk of hearings reports is enormous because legislators frequently do not wish to listen to long, detailed expositions and simply say, "Just insert your presentation in the record." Thus, the proceedings of a hearing often contain reprints of all the essential material relevant to a particular issue. These reports are available selectively in depository libraries, from the Government Printing Office (for a fee), and sometimes *free* from the chairperson of a committee *while the hearings are in progress or until the initial supply is exhausted.*

To obtain hearings reports, it is important to cite them correctly. The citation should include:

1. U.S. Congress
2. The part of Congress (Senate or House)
3. The subcommittee (if any)
4. The committee

5. The title of the hearing

6. The number of the Congress (93rd, 94th, etc.)

7. The session

See the example on page 64.

The sources for identifying current hearings are the following: *The Congressional Information Service Index*. Washington, D.C.: Congressional Information Service, 1970–. (Page 102.)

The Monthly Catalogue of U.S. Government Publications and its cumulations. Hamden, Conn.: Shoe String Press, 1973–. (Page 29.)

The sources for identifying past hearings are *Cumulative Index of Congressional Committee Hearings (Not Confidential in Character) Second Quadrennial Supplement from the Eighty-Eighth Congress (January 3, 1963) through the Eighty-Ninth Congress (January 3, 1967) together with Committee Prints in the United States Senate Library.* (Compiled by Carmen Carpenter under the direction of F. R. Valeo. Washington, D.C.: Government Printing Office, 1967.)

Cumulative Index of Congressional Committee Hearings (Not Confidential in Character) Third Quadrennial Supplement from the Ninetieth Congress (January 10, 1967) through the Ninety-First Congress (January 2, 1971) together with Selected Committee Prints in the United States Senate Library. (Compiled by Carmen Carpenter and Polly Sargent under the direction of F. R. Valeo. Washington, D.C.: Government Printing Office, 1971.)

Bills of Congress.

Before a law is enacted, it is called a bill. Bills can be primary data for one studying the legislative process. Bills come with the following designations:

H.R. (bill from the House of Representatives)

S. (bill from the Senate)

H. Res. or S. Res. (House resolution or Senate resolution)

H. J. Res. or S. J. Res. (Joint resolutions, depending upon origin)

H. Con. Res. or S. Con. Res. (Concurrent resolutions, depending upon origin)

Digest of Public General Bills and Selected Resolutions with Index. Washington, D.C.: Government Printing Office, 1936–.

Designated by congressional session and issue number, this digest is the legislative product of a session of Congress. It is especially valuable because it includes a digest and legislative history of each measure receiving action, the date reported, the report number, the date of debate, etc. With this information, you can read the debate on the measure in the *Congressional Record,* check the vote, etc. This digest also contains an author or sponsor index, so you can see what bills a particular member introduced, and a subject matter index.

Calendars of the United States House of Representatives and History of Legislation.

These are published daily during each session with a cumulative volume at the end of the session. For the House (the Senate has a calendar, but it is much less elaborate), the calendar is the daily plan of work. On Monday it contains a cumulative legislative history of each pending bill and a subject matter index on pending legislation. Its primary use is that of a status report during the session, i.e., what is being considered and where, when, and how.

Congressional Serial Set. Washington, D.C.: Government Printing Office, 1817–.

This set of 13,500 volumes is a collection of the above mentioned documents, containing House and Senate journals, documents, and reports. It does not include bills, hearings, laws, or "committee prints." The reports are committee reports and are especially important in that they contain not only brief summaries of the hearings but also the individual views of the committee members who participated. Committee reports usually contain the best brief summary of all the important facts and arguments concerning the bill in question.

Obviously, it can be difficult to trace a document through 13,500 volumes, so the following indexes, all published by the Government Printing Office, can help one find a particular item.

> *Checklist of United States Public Documents, 1789-1909.* (Washington, D.C.: Government Printing Office, 1911; reprinted, New York: Kraus Reprint Co., 1962).
>
> *Catalog of the Public Documents of Congress, 1893-1940.* (Washington, D.C.: Government Printing Office, published irregularly between 1896 and 1945).
>
> *Decennial Cumulative Index 1941-1950.* 2 vols. (Washington, D.C.: Government Printing Office, 1953). This has been supplemented by an index series published yearly, *Numerical Lists and Schedules of Volumes of the Reports and Documents* for each session of Congress.

The Monthly Catalog of United States Government Publications lists each volume as it is sent to the depository libraries, and is, itself, sent to each library as an index. These "depository libraries" are usually located at the state universities in the larger cities of every state.

Congressional Quarterly Service

Although privately printed since 1945, the "CQ" series of publications has achieved the status of an official publication and is the most frequently cited source of congressional information. Its major attribute is its concise factual arrangement of material previously tucked away in bulky government documents.

The Congressional Quarterly publications present a careful review of each session of Congress in both legislative and political areas. Facts, figures, and unbiased commentary on all aspects of congressional activity are presented, including committee meetings and floor action. The President's position on all major legislation and roll-call votes in Congress are super-imposed. Also included are the President's messages to Congress, his news conferences, his vetoes, and so on.

The basic publication of the service is the *Congressional Quarterly Weekly Report*. From this report a yearly *Congressional Quarterly Almanac* is compiled.

Congress and the Nation is a hard-bound volume documenting all major congressional and presidential actions and national political campaigns for the twenty-year period from 1945 to 1964. Volume 2, covering the Johnson years (1965-1968), was published in 1969. A volume for 1969 to 1973 was published in 1974.

Congressional Quarterly also publishes semiannually a current handbook for the study of American government, the *Congressional Quarterly Guide to Current American Government*, which contains research material written and arranged for classroom and study use, as well as the *Editorial Research Reports*, a weekly publication that objectively assembles the facts involved in current controversial topics in well-researched and documented articles of about six thousand words each. A library subscribing to the *Congressional Quarterly Weekly Report* probably also receives the *Editorial Research Reports* (page 150).

National Journal. Burt Hoffman, ed. Washington, D.C.: Center for Political Research, 1970–.

This journal was founded by a group of editors and reporters who left Congressional Quarterly because they felt it did not pay enough attention to bureaucratic decision making. The *Journal* is published weekly and designed as a monitor of all government actions. It does more than record government actions; it analyzes all the details surrounding such actions, focusing mainly on the relationships between the various power-wielding agencies that cram the nation's capital. The interests involved in any issue are plainly identified—this, in itself, cuts away much of the arcanum for the student. It also contains in-depth reports on federal programs, biographical

information on government officials, and analyses of congressional districts.

Office of the President

Weekly Compilation of Presidential Documents. Washington,
D.C.: Government Printing Office, 1965–.

Published every Monday under the auspices of the Office
of the Federal Register, National Archives and Records Service,
and General Services Administration, this source contains the
presidential materials released by the White House up to 5 P.M.
the preceding Friday. It includes the President's addresses,
remarks, announcements, appointments and nominations, executive orders, memoranda, meetings with foreign leaders, and
proclamations, as well as reports to the President. These reports
are becoming more informal. For example, the issue for the last
week of the Nixon presidency is especially interesting.

Federal Register. Washington, D.C.: Government Printing Office, 1936–.

Published five times a week, the *Federal Register* includes
presidential executive orders, proclamations, reorganization
plans, and rules and regulations issued by executive departments
and agencies. It is accurate and complete.

The Judiciary

United States Reports. Washington, D.C.: Government Printing
Office, 1790–.

This is a compilation of each decision rendered by the
United States Supreme Court. Most decisions include majority,
dissenting, and concurring opinions. These opinions contain the
sweep of facts, attitudes, and legal concepts relating to the
important issues that come before the Supreme Court.

United States Code and *United States Statutes At Large.* Washington, D.C.: Government Printing Office, 1875–.

The *United States Code* is published every six years, with
an annual supplement. This is the source to consult for a paper

on any legislation that has been passed by Congress. It is the source of up-to-date public laws covering every topic. Another source for public laws is *United States Statutes At Large,* a study that breaks down the public laws into two parts: first, all public laws that were passed during a particular year; and second, all private bills passed in that year. Laws in both books are classified under fifty titles, such as public lands, education, defense, Congress, and banks.

There are also commercially published editions of the *Code* known as *United States Code Annotated* (St. Paul, Minn.: West, 1927–) and *Federal Code Annotated* (New York & Indianapolis, Ind.: Bobbs-Merrill, 1937–). These annotated editions include notes on judicial interpretations of the law as well as the law itself. If available, they are more useful than the *United States Code.*

If one is interested in state rather than federal laws, the proper source would be individual state codes.

Governmental and Political Process

All About Politics. Paul A. Theis and William L. Steponkus. New York: R. R. Bowker Co., 1972.

This is a book of questions and answers about a variety of political topics. It is most useful as a "question raiser" or topic selector.

Canadian Annual Review of Politics and Public Affairs. John Saywell, ed. Toronto, Ont., and Buffalo, N.Y.: University of Toronto Press, 1960–.

This contains definitive essays on important aspects of Canadian government and politics. It covers Parliament, federal/ provincial relations, the parties, each province, external affairs, and the economy. It is a good first stop for a paper on Canada.

American Government Annual. New York: Holt, Rinehart & Winston, 1958-1968.

This contains timely essays by political scientists on topics current when they were written about. Examples: "Religion and Politics, 1960-65"; "Congress, 1963."

Dictionary of the History of Ideas: Studies of Selected Pivotal Ideas. Philip P. Wiener, ed. New York: Charles Scribner, 1973.

Although many of the entries fall outside the realm of politics, there are many that deal in a multidisciplinary fashion with a number of key political concepts. "Authority," for example, is traced from ancient times to the present, and the many issues raised by the concept are thoroughly examined.

Electoral Behavior, A Comparative Handbook. Richard Rose. New York: The Free Press, 1974.

Today, political behavior is no longer considered in isolation from socioeconomic and cultural factors. This valuable source summarizes such data from Western nations. Essays approach the frontier of the interdisciplinary study of political behavior. An article on Italy, for example, deals with social-psychological influences, contradictions in Italian political behavior, consumption patterns, and life-styles.

The Future of the Future. John McHale. New York: George Braziller, 1969.

This book examines the context, issues, methodology, and problems of studying the future. It is readable and useful for the study of a variety of current political problems.

Handbook of Political Psychology. Jeanne N. Knutson. San Francisco: Jossey Bass, 1973.

What influences political behavior? Most psychologists agree that the list of factors would include those items that influence all behavior. These sophisticated essays illustrate the interface between psychology and politics, i.e., personality, political attitudes, socialization, the authoritarian personality, patterns of leadership, aggression, revolution, and war.

How Democracies Vote. Enid Lakeman, ed. London: Faber & Faber, 1970.

The American electoral system is not the only possible one for a democracy. This source outlines the myriad of systems, such as proportional representation, used throughout the world. It is especially useful on the practical implications of each system in terms of who benefits.

Human Behavior: An Inventory of Scientific Findings. Bernard Berelson and Gary Steiner. New York: Harcourt Brace Jovanovich, 1964.

Inventory is the key word in this title. This is an easy-to-read inventory of hundreds of propositions about human behavior, many of which can be related to political behavior. Each research finding is concisely explored and illustrated. Examples of findings: people with well-adjusted personalities are more likely to be active politically; class is more important in determining political views in urban than in rural areas.

The Political Marketplace. David L. Rosenbloom, ed. New York: Quadrangle, 1972.

Among other things, politics and elections are now a business. This source includes the name, address, and phone number as of 1972 of every elected national and state official and many local and party officials. In addition, there are indexes to that new actor on the political scene, the campaign consultant, campaign material companies, campaign planning assistance, campaign laws, etc.

Political Science Annual: An International Review. Indianapolis, Ind.: Bobbs-Merrill, 1966–.

This work is patterned after annual reviews of research that have flourished in the natural sciences for many years. These essays focus primarily on the discipline of political science and only secondarily on the political phenomenon being studied. The volumes are useful for advanced students who want to understand the state of the discipline at a particular time. Examples: conflicting conceptions of political violence; American political parties, an interpretation with four analytic levels.

Problems of Government and Politics

Civil Rights: A Current Guide to People, Organizations, and Events. John A. Adams and Joan M. Burke. New York: R. R. Bowker, 1970.

The civil rights revolution of the last two decades has been a momentous event in American politics. This source includes the membership, objectives, and activities of the major civil rights organizations; biographical sketches; and a detailed chronology of events.

Congressional Digest. Washington, D.C.: Congressional Digest Corp., 1921–.

This privately printed monthly publication explores both sides of current controversial topics. After an opening statement of the question under discussion, pro and con arguments drawn from the opinions of world experts in that particular field are advanced. In the July 1975 issue, for example, the battle raged over the question of extending the Voting Rights Act.

Editorial Research Reports (Congressional Quarterly). Hoyt Gimlin, ed. Washington, D.C.: Congressional Quarterly, 1923–.

Issued weekly, this publication selects a major issue currently receiving public attention and assembles the facts. Each report starts with a recital of upcoming or recent developments. That is followed by an exposition of the main arguments on both sides and a list of the forces at work to change the situation. Also included are further background, historical development, and proposals for the future. Moreover, there are approximately 10 one-page summaries of other issues of the week. Although designed for newspaper editorial writers, *Editorial Research Reports* provides an excellent one-stop summary of current issues.

A Dictionary of Modern Revolutions. Edward S. Hyams. New York: Taplinger, 1973.

The authors quote Baudelaire, who said, "Life being what it is, one dreams of revenge." This is a guide to how these dreams have become a reality. The entries tend to be long and philosophical, ranging from Marx to the Soledad Brothers.

Issues before the General Assemblies of the United Nations: 1946-1965. New York: Arno, 1970.

This is a specially compiled selection of excerpts from the major speeches and issues on the General Assembly agenda since its first session in 1946. Also compiled for this edition is a cumulative index that allows the student to find in one source basic information concerning relevant problems facing the United Nations—a good "first stop" for a term paper.

Money and Politics: Contributions, Campaign Abuses, and the Law. Lester A. Sobel, ed. New York: Facts on File, 1974.

This is a concise factual summary of the revelations since 1972. It includes an especially useful summary of the Watergate Hearings, important contributions, Nixon's homes, etc.

Public Policy, An Annual Yearbook. The John Fitzgerald Kennedy School of Government, Harvard University. Cambridge, Mass.: Harvard University Press, 1940.

Each issue contains scholarly articles about practical problems, ranging over many topics. This became the quarterly periodical *Public Policy* in 1969 (p. 234).

The Urban Affairs Annual Reviews. Beverly Hills, Calif.: Sage, 1967–.

These are yearbooks on practical matters of government and administration. Each volume focuses on a particular problem such as "Improving the Quality of Urban Management." Authors tend to be administrators, consultants, or academicians with a problem-solving orientation.

Vital Speeches of the Day. New York: City News, 1934–.

This monthly journal prints verbatim important speeches (usually in full) of recognized leaders of public opinion in America. Generally, it covers both sides of public questions, thereby offering the significant thought of leading minds on current national problems. The journal explains that its purpose is to offer students "the finest textbook material . . . from those who have attained leadership in the fields of politics, economics, education, sociology, government, criminology, finance, business, taxation, health, law, labor. . . ."

Your Government and the Environment: An Environmental Digest, Volume III. Matthew J. Kerbec. Arlington, Va.: Output Systems, 1973-74.

The environment issue is immensely complex. This guide pulls together the whole policy area with readable essays on each area of pollution, changes in laws, new scientific findings, grant policies, and monitoring techniques.

Ideas and Values in the Political Process

Encyclopedia of Philosophy. Paul Edwards, ed. New York: Macmillan, 1967.

Many political philosophers also concern themselves with philosophical questions in the areas of ethics, scientific method, the nature of reality, etc. To understand their political ideas, it is often helpful to view the other areas of their thought. This in-depth source will help you do that. Articles are lengthy and scholarly, so the book might be difficult for the beginning student.

A Glossary of Political Ideas. Maurice Cranston and Sanford A. Lakoff. New York: Basic Books, 1969.

This is an unusually useful source for starting a term paper. Over fifty key ideas are explained and analyzed. Liberalism, for example, has meant different things at different times from the era of John Stuart Mill to the present. This volume traces those meanings and then presents a short bibliography for future reference.

Great Books of the Western World and The Great Ideas. A Syntopicon. Mortimer J. Adler, ed. Chicago: Encyclopaedia Britannica, 1961.

The two-volume *Syntopicon* contains an analytic essay for each of the 102 "great ideas." These essays break down and analyze each idea, illustrating in the process the intellectual handles of each. Under "law," for instance, is a clear and succinct approach to the idea of law—divine and natural law, and the relationship of law and the individual. The remaining fifty-four volumes contain the works of the great thinkers and writers of Western civilization. To these fifty-four volumes the essays of the *Syntopicon* are keyed, permitting one to trace the development of an idea through history or to compare the views of two or more giants of history. Each of the 102 essays is cross-indexed, providing innumerable approaches to a single subject.

The Great Ideas Today. Mortimer J. Adler. Chicago: Encyclopaedia Britannica, 1961–.

Each year the *Great Ideas* volumes are brought up to date with articles by leading scholars and world figures. In the 1971 book, Marshall Cohen relates current practice and the meaning of modern ideas of civil disobedience to some of the great ideas of the past.

Masterpieces of World Philosophy in Summary Form. Frank N. Magill, ed. New York: Harper & Row, 1963.

Some academicians feel that students of philosophy or political theory must gain their understanding from the original works of the philosophers themselves with little or no outside assistance. There is room for disagreement. While it is always beneficial to read the original, most students can help sharpen their understanding by outside direction. A glance at one of the summaries offered is likely to raise the student's level of comprehension. Also, there are times when it is neither wise nor possible to read an entire work, in which case this reference can save the day.

Sources of Democracy: Voices of Freedom, Hope, and Justice. Saul K. Padover, New York: McGraw-Hill, 1973.

This work contains ideas, documents, and statements about democracy with special applied sections on current problem areas such as justice and race relations. It is a good first stop for an idea paper.

The Political Science Reviewer: An Annual Review of Books. Bryn Mawr, Pa: Intercollegiate's Studies Institute, 1971—.

Although presented as a series of book reviews, this source contains lengthy philosophical essays going well beyond the boundaries of usual book reviews. Less than ten books are reviewed per issue. Each review is useful as an idea piece.

Guides to Action in the Political Process

The Compact Guide to Parliamentary Procedure. Harvey Cromwell. New York: Crowell, 1973.

While *Roberts Rules of Order* remains the basic source in this field, this handy guide provides quick, on-the-spot information on how to put questions on the floor, arrange seconds, reconsider, etc.

A Citizen's Guide to Air Pollution. David Bates. New York: McGraw-Hill, 1972.

This book describes what causes pollution and what can be done about it. It compares existing standards, recommends new standards, and outlines proposed legislation.

FINDING A JOB

Federal Career Directory: A Guide for College Students. United States Civil Service Commission. Washington, D.C.: Government Printing Office, 1956—.

This is one of a dozen or so guides to federal employment. The commission's regional offices also publish separate local guides.

POLITICAL ACTION

A Is A: Libertarian Directory. Dale Haviland. Brighton, Mich.: Mega, 1972.

Libertarianism is a growing political movement in the United States. Although it includes many cleavages and points of view, its proponents generally support individual rights, personal liberty, and laissez-faire capitalism. This is both a philosophical explanation of libertarianism and a practical guide to other sources, individuals, and organizations dedicated to libertarian principles.

Environment U.S.A.: A Guide to Agencies, People, and Resources. The Onyx Group, Inc., ed., Glenn L. Paulson, adv. ed. New York: R. R. Bowker, 1974.

The ecological revolution has spawned a whole host of groups and programs. This work contains both useful essays on the laws and policies and an exhaustive directory of the participants in environmental policy.

How to Get Things Changed: A Handbook for Tackling Community Problems. Bert Strauss and Mary E. Stowe. Garden City, N.Y.: Doubleday, 1974.

The authors base their experience on a federally sponsored community-change project in Virginia. The special values of the book are the concrete suggestions for accomplishing the nitty-gritty aspects of community change, i.e., the idea of using a facilitator rather than a chairman for a meeting, strategies of organization, etc. The book can also be useful for an academic . research paper as a framework or criterion for examining other change efforts.

The Population Activist's Handbook. The Population Institute. New York: Macmillan, 1974.

Theorizing about population control is one thing—doing something about it is another. The first section in this source focuses on action; it deals with policy, political tactics, how to work with office holders, etc. The second section deals with the use of research as an action tactic and tells how to conduct polls, surveys, etc. as a step toward awareness and resolution of the population problem. Section three deals with actual change tactics—such as how to set up services related to abortion, VD, etc. The worldwide implications of the population problem are discussed in the last section.

The Rights of Students: The Basic ACLU Guide to a Student's Rights. Alan Levine, Eve Cary, and Diane Divoky. New York: Sunrise/Dutton, 1973.

Although this source was published before the passage of the landmark 1974 act that gives students access to their school records, it is still a valuable source. The topics include all the major aspects of student life—those related to education as well as a number of other life situations encountered by students such as marriage, pregnancy, etc.

The Rights of Women: The Basic ACLU Guide to Woman's Rights. Susan C. Ross. New York: Sunrise/Dutton, 1973.

One way to learn how a system works is to try to change it. This source explains the American legal system and simultaneously helps women to exercise their rights. In addition to the expected legal explanations, the source includes a directory of women's organizations.

Working on the System: A Comprehensive Manual for Citizen Access to Federal Agencies. James R. Michael, ed. Ralph Nader's Center for the Study of Responsive Law. New York: Basic Books, 1974.

Political scientists have spent much more time studying the inner workings of Congress than they have on the bureaucracy. The action-oriented Nader groups have more than made up for this. This source pulls together much of the work of Ralph

Nader and his various groups for the past ten years. Although the book is typically written in journalistic style and is action-oriented, it contains a great deal of very basic information that is available nowhere else. The main thrusts are how bureaucratic agencies operate; how to get information about—and from—them, both officially and unofficially; how they use administrative procedure; and how you can use it for your purposes. There is also a series of lengthy chapters on individual agencies.

Additional Specialized Research Guides

Confidential Information Sources: Public and Private. John Carroll. Los Angeles: Security World, 1975.

John Carroll has spent a lifetime as a private investigator. This book is a guide to the *legal* use of a wide variety of information sources including motor vehicle records, the Internal Revenue Service, the Census Bureau, etc.

Directory of Information Resources in the United States. The National Referral Center for Science and Technology of the Library of Congress. Washington, D.C.: Government Printing Office, published irregularly.

To obtain material from this source, it is necessary to know precisely what you want. This directory contains what librarians term "fugitive material," in that it is available to the public on request only, and when the supply is exhausted it is unobtainable. This guide will supply a list of most federal and federally sponsored agencies (such as the East-West Center of the University of Hawaii), and will describe their activities and the type of data available from each. Most of the material comes in the form of printed government documents and in typewritten and mimeographed reports. To date, only five volumes of the directory have been published, two of which are particularly helpful to the political science student: *Social Sciences* (1965) and *Federal Government* (1967).

A Guide to Library Sources in Political Science: American Government. Clement E. Vose. Washington, D.C.: American Political Science Association, 1975.

This is the first in a series of specialized monographs on library sources. It is unusual in that it is truly a work of original scholarship about library sources. Various sources such as dictionaries and encyclopedias are compared and analyzed with reference to individual items.

A Guide to Legal Research. Erwin C. Surrency, Benjamin Feld, and Joseph Crea. New York: Oceana, 1959.

This guide discusses legal research for the nonlawyer. It contains clear step-by-step procedures for tracing decisions, finding statutes, etc.

Guide to Reference Material in Political Science. Lubomyr R. Wynar. Denver, Col.: Bibliographic Institute, 1966.

This reference consists of two volumes of a conventionally organized and extensively annotated guide to bibliographies. Generally, it provides an acceptable basic bibliography for the major fields of political science.

Guide to the Study of International Relations. J. K. Zawodny. San Francisco: Chandler, 1966.

This guide is a paperback volume designed to aid the student and researcher find the widely scattered and often complex materials tied to the study of international relations—government documents, national archives materials, UN publications, and up-to-date, empirically validated findings in the behavioral sciences. It holds more than five hundred cross-indexed entries classified under subject headings that, except for the journals, have been annotated and can guide students efficiently through several million titles to the specific one they desire.

Guide to Reference Books. Constance M. Winchell. 8th ed. Chicago: American Library Association, 1967.

The most comprehensive of all guides of this type, the *Guide to Reference Books* was first published in 1902 and through eight editions and supplements has remained conspicuously up-to-date. The latest edition divides 7,500 titles into five categories: general reference works; humanities; social sciences; history and area studies; and the pure and applied sciences.

How to Locate Educational Information and Data. Carter Alexander and Arvid J. Burke. 4th ed. rev. New York: Teachers College Press, 1958.

Although it is directed toward the education major, this handbook's basic instruction in the use of the library should benefit other students as well. It describes reference sources, card catalogs, periodical indexes, bibliographies, and government documents, enabling students to locate the information that they require.

The Literature of Political Science. Clifton Brock. New York: R. R. Bowker, 1969.

This is the most thorough of all the political science guides. It contains a very useful guide to congressional documents and social science periodicals.

A Reader's Guide to the Social Sciences. Bert F. Hoselitz, ed. Rev. ed. Glencoe, Ill.: The Free Press, 1970.

This is broken down into sections on history, geography, sociology, anthropology, psychology, economics, and political science. The last chapter is written by Heinz Eulau, who presents a splendid introduction to the more important studies in political science.

Sources of Information in the Social Sciences: A Guide to Literature. 2nd ed. Carl M. White et al. Chicago: American Library Association, 1973.

Besides general reference works, this source offers separate treatments for history, economics and business administration, sociology, anthropology, psychology, education, and political science. Each chapter is complete with introduction, important studies, bibliographies, and data sources. The volume is geared for the interdisciplinary and behavioral approach to the social sciences.

The World of Learning. London: Europa, 1947–.

This book contains basic descriptions, and a list of responsible individuals in a worldwide directory of colleges, universities, research institutes, museums, libraries, and archives is also included. It has a first-rate index that allows one to identify all the organizations involved in each area of interest.

Washington IV: A Comprehensive Directory of the Nation's Capital People and Institutions. Cary Grayson, Jr. and Susan Lukowski, eds. Washington, D.C.: Potomac, 1975.

This excellent one-stop guide to the nation's capital includes international, national, state, and local agencies headquartered in the District of Columbia. It also lists embassies, private and nonprofit organizations such as American Civil Liberties Union, press, TV, radio, private clubs, lawyers associations, labor unions, research associations, foundations, and numerous community groups. If you are coming to Washington, this book can save you much valuable time and lead you to the right organization to answer your questions.

Washington Information Directory. Washington Congressional Quarterly, 1975.

This directory covers both Washington and federal regional offices. It is especially helpful in that it organizes both government and private information sources by subject with current addresses and phone numbers of key officials.

PART THREE

5

Additional Information for the Student of Political Science

WRITING A LETTER TO THE EDITOR

Most newspapers have a letter-to-the-editor column, which they run as they see fit—once a week, several times a week, or daily.

This is one way of corresponding with your representatives in Washington and your state capital. It is also an excellent way of shaking out an issue within the circulation area of the newspaper; chances are, your letter will draw pro and con responses from your fellow readers. And it has been said that, when your letter appears in print, the chances are strong that you are addressing the largest audience you will ever have in your life.

Here are a few tips to help your letter find its way past the editor's desk and into print:

1. If possible, use a typewriter, double space, and type on only one side of the paper.
2. Be clear and as brief as possible. If you ramble on for five hundred words, your letter is sure to be cut drastically, and you might even lose the chance to get into print.

3. Focus on a single topic per letter; make sure it is timely, even newsworthy.

4. Hone that first sentence to a good edge; grab the editor's attention quickly.

5. If you are criticizing, take some of the sting out of your complaint by adding a word of praise, appreciation, or agreement. End the letter with some constructive suggestions.

6. Be calm. Do not rant or use abusive or violent language. That is cause for an automatic rejection in most newspapers.

7. Do not hesitate to bring moral judgments to bear on the issue you are tackling. Appeal to the reader's sense of fair play, justice, and even mercy.

8. You can make a few language changes in your letter and, in that way, send it to editors of newspapers in other cities. You should change the language a little because many metropolitan newspapers (most notably the *New York Times*) will not publish a letter that has also been sent to other papers.

9. Always sign your name and give your address and phone number as the letter will, in all probability, be verified. You may use a pen name, but the editor must know the source of the letter.

10. Do not despair if your letter is not printed the same week it was mailed. And do not be utterly discouraged if it is never printed. At least the editor saw it and now has the benefit of your views on the topic. So—try again.

CORRESPONDING WITH GOVERNMENT OFFICIALS

Writing Tips

Rep. Morris K. Udall, (D. Ariz.) and the League of Women Voters have provided these hints on how to write to a member of Congress.

1. Write to your own senator or congressperson only. Letters written to others will eventually end up on the desk of your representative anyway.
2. Write at the proper time, when a bill is being discussed or on the floor.
3. Use your own words and your own stationery. Avoid signing and sending a form or mimeographed letter.
4. Do not be a pen pal; do not try to instruct the representative on every issue that arises.
5. Do not demand a commitment before all the facts are in. Bills rarely become law in the same form in which they are introduced.
6. Identify all bills by their title or their number.
7. If possible, include pertinent editorials from local newspapers.
8. Be constructive. If a bill deals with a problem that you admit exists, but you believe the bill is the wrong approach, tell what you think the right approach should be.
9. If you have expert knowledge or wide experience in a particular area, share it with the appropriate person. But do not pretend to wield vast political influence.
10. Write to a member of Congress when the legislator does something you approve of, too. A note of appreciation will make you be remembered more favorably the next time.
11. Feel free to write when you have a question or problem dealing with procedures of government departments.
12. Ask to be put on the mailing list for the newsletter. Most representatives today distribute newsletters and often send questionnaires soliciting constituents' opinions.
13. A telegram is an attention getter and is especially effective just before a vote. It is also easy to send. Just lift your phone and send a one-dollar, fifteen-word Public Opinion Message.

14. Finally, be brief, write legibly, and be sure to use the proper form of address.

Correct Form for Writing to Government Officials

President
    The President
    The White House
    Washington, D.C. 20500

    Dear Mr. President:
    Very respectfully yours,

Vice-President
    The Vice-President
    The White House
    Washington, D.C. 20500

    Dear Mr. Vice-President:
    Sincerely yours,

Senator
    The Honorable [Full Name]
    United States Senate
    Washington, D.C. 20510

    Dear Senator [Name]:
    Sincerely yours,

Representative
    The Honorable [Full Name]
    House of Representatives
    Washington, D.C. 20515

    Dear Mr. [Name]:
    Sincerely yours,

Member of the Cabinet
    The Honorable [Full Name]
    The Secretary of the Treasury
    Washington, D.C. 20520

    Dear Mr. Secretary:
    Sincerely yours,

OBTAINING GOVERNMENT INFORMATION: THE FREEDOM OF INFORMATION ACT

The basic rule since July 4, 1966, when Lyndon Johnson signed the Freedom of Information Act into law, is that government information *is available* and the burden of proof falls on the government to prove why you should *not* have it, not upon you to prove why you should. Agencies must publish in the *Federal Register*:

1. General procedures on where and how to obtain information from that agency
2. Rules, policies, and statements regarding the obtaining of information

(This material may be more easily available in the *Code of Federal Regulations*, but there is approximately a one-year time lag between publication in the *Register* and in the *Code*.)

The point here obviously is to prevent a government employee from making up rules on the spot to prevent you from obtaining information.

The following information an agency *must* make available in public reading rooms or put on sale:

1. The results of administrative cases and rulings
2. Statements of policy not appearing in the *Federal Register*
3. Administrative staff manuals that affect members of the public

Agencies are instructed to make this information available promptly and at a reasonable cost.

Exceptions

There are, however, nine categories of information exempted from this act:

1. Records classified as secret, top secret, or confidential (You can, however, request such records with the classified sections deleted.)
2. Internal rules and procedures
3. Matters specifically exempted by statute
4. Trade secrets
5. Internal communications

6. Personal and medical files

7. Some investigatory records such as certain FBI files

8. Records regarding the regulation of a financial institution

9. Geological and geophysical information

The greatest difficulty in using this act is in locating the records. Both the *United States Government Manual* (p. 130) and the *Congressional Directory* (p. 112) can be of help in locating the proper agency. Then it is up to you to describe what you want as accurately as possible. If the material you seek is in a printed document, there is, of course, no problem. You simply need to know that something occurred (i.e., a research report was written by a particular person) in order to request it.

The following letter taken from *Your Right to Government Information: How to Use the FOIA* (American Civil Liberties Union, 22 East 40th Street, New York, New York, 10016) illustrates the basic approach in requesting information:

Secretary of Defense
Department of Defense
Washington, D.C.

Dear Sir:

I wish to obtain a copy of a study of the Viet Cong which was commissioned by the Department of Defense and conducted by Lawrence Albert Newberry, a psychologist. The study is based on interviews by Mr. Newberry with 49 Viet Cong and North Vietnamese deserters in Viet Nam between 1967 and August 1971, and concludes that high ideological motivation has been responsible for the military successes of the Viet Cong.

I have devoted much of my academic career to the study of American involvement in Southeast Asia, particularly Viet Nam. Accordingly, the results of Mr. Newberry's research, which are currently in the sole possession of the Department of Defense, are extremely important to my work. I therefore formally request, pursuant to Title 5, United States Code, Section 552(a) (3), and the First Amendment to the United States Constitution, that you make promptly available to me a copy of Mr. Newberry's study of the Viet Cong. Please contact me immediately if you have any questions about further identification of the records.

If for any reason it is believed that portions of this report are exempt from disclosure under the Freedom of Information Act, initially I consent to a sanitized copy, deleting any such allegedly exempt material. This initial consent is designed to obtain the documents requested as quickly as possible, and in no way waives my right to the entire study which I may still choose to press.

I look forward to hearing from you within the next 10 working days, pursuant to Section (a) (6) (i) of the Freedom of Information Act. In the event I am denied any material, please specify the statutory basis for the denial and the names and titles of the persons responsible for this decision.

> Yours very truly,
> John Doe
> Professor of Politics
> Princeton University

For further details, write the ACLU for a copy of this brochure and see *Working on the System* (p. 156).

A SHORTHAND SYSTEM FOR MARKING UP BOOKS

The authors firmly believe in marking up one's own books. A book is a research tool and can be made even more useful if it bears some record of impressions from previous readings. Consequently, a shorthand system may be suggested that quickly and neatly reminds the researcher of judgments of various materials in the book. This shorthand, or symbolic retrieval, system may include signs, symbols, numbers, or any device the researcher can easily recognize. The following are simply examples of what may be done. Your own system will undoubtedly be highly personalized.

1. * for important; ** for very important
2. F for fact
3. T for theory
4. P for principle
5. ? for doubtful
6. S for suggestive
7. Cf. (compare) as in cf. Plato, *Republic II.*

    8. Incl. for include in research paper

    9. Q, or Par. for quote or paraphrase in the paper

  10. X for the researcher not being sure of the value of the author's point

Such signs written in the margin of a book can and ought to be combined. E.g., *F means an important fact; ?PcfFord means a doubtful principle that is to be compared or contrasted to the Ford approach or principle in the same matter. This sort of shorthand may also be used in one's notebook to annotate class notes and then to quickly glean the material to be included in the research paper.

DEVELOPING A BOOK REPORT

Evaluating the Book

Usually the student is required to evaluate and report on books that have been assigned. The *date* of publication of a book may be very important. That is to say, *when* the book was written is the key to the *stage* of discussion of a given topic. For example, a book on moon topography published in the 1950s, before man visited the moon, would be of considerably less value than one written today. Too, the name of the *publisher* may offer some hint as to where the writer is from and what his biases and points of view are. For certain publishers specialize in books written from a certain viewpoint or champion certain schools of thought.

Moreover, the author's *preface* or an *introduction* by a known authority will usually supply clues to the orientation and scope of the work. The *table of contents* offers further clues, as does a scanning of the *footnote-bibliography* sections. And just as important in this regard is the *index*, if there is one. If, for example, a book entitled *Ancient Philosophies* contains many references to Plato and only a few to Aristotle, you may assume that the author has been more influenced by Plato then by Aristotle. Similarly, if the index holds many references to

Christian writers, it is safe to assume that the author is viewing his topic from a Christian viewpoint.

If a book you will use as a source has been reviewed, by all means read the *reviews* before tackling the book. There are several reasons for this. First, the reviewer is professionally bound to have identified the main points; in addition, he probably will have noted the author's adherence to or departure from traditional approaches; finally, you may wish to cite the opinion(s) of the reviewer in your paper.

The more expert the researcher becomes in the general area of political science (and in dealing with intellectual materials in general), the more efficiently and instinctively he will be able to evaluate a book on politics. Nevertheless, for the tyro in political science research, there are various guidelines to help him or her decide the worth and reliability of a book. Foremost of these are the publisher and the author.

Is the publisher of the book in question reputable? The university presses usually publish material of a high academic quality, and the more prestigious the university, the more likely the book is to be authoritative. Then, too, certain series of books have a reputation for accuracy and reliability.

Now, what is the author's reputation? If it is strong in the field in which he or she is writing, then you most likely can relax with the conclusions drawn. But should the author be writing on politics from a dais of theater (e.g., Richard Burton on the pathology of politics) then the conclusions are at least suspect. For this reason, it is wise to consult *Who's Who*, or some similar reference, if the author is unknown to you. Beyond this, does the author's viewpoint, even in a field of expertise, affect the usefulness of the conclusions? It is vitally important to know the general position the author holds, especially in areas of controversy, for a political philosopher from the analytic, Anglo-Saxon school will approach a problem far differently than a political philosopher from the continental European school. Doctrinal and factional considerations may mean that a recognized authority in one of these traditions may be considered unhelpful in another.

For the student, all this can be bewildering. It is a difficult task to sort out the intrinsic value of the work. But when one becomes competent enough, certain assumptions and approaches will be elevated, cataloged, or discarded. Until then, the neophyte in political science cannot afford the luxury of facile judgments but must consider all these legitimate and provisionally valuable.

Here are some specific ways to form a judgment about a book's value:

1. Read the table of contents and the index. What is suggested in the table of contents as the topic and approach of the work?
2. If there is a preface, does it pinpoint the scope and concerns of the author?
3. Does the index reflect an overbalance in one direction or another of any of several schools of thought on the topic?
4. Does the book deal with a field generally, or does it zero in on your research topic?
5. Is the author without prejudice, discussing opponents fairly and at length? Is the argument based on opinion or on fact? Is the logic of the argument sound? Are objections to the stated position considered? Does the author depend on reliable authorities? Do footnoting and bibliography seem appropriate? And finally, does the effectiveness of the presentation depend on literary charm rather than on the substantive aspects of information and argument?

FALLACIES IN LOGIC TO WATCH FOR

If a book is to be convincing, it must be logical. And we must be able to recognize such fallacies in the author's logic as insufficient evidence; unreasonable extrapolation; the non sequitur; post hoc, ergo propter hoc; the distorted example; the red herring; the circular argument; and the practice of begging the question. We will tackle each of them briefly here.

An argument may be controversial if there is *insufficient evidence* to convince others of its truth. That is, a writer must give enough essential and specific support to convince a reader that the contentions are valid and are founded in reality.

Extrapolation is a surmise based on past events that suggests certain future courses of action. And *unreasonable extrapolation* is such a prediction that does not take all existing conditions into consideration, thereby rendering the prediction invalid.

Non sequitur is a Latin phrase that means "it does not follow." It occurs when too many steps and too much information have been omitted from an argument, causing a lack of relationship between supporting statements and conclusions.

Post hoc, ergo propter hoc is a special type of *non sequitur*. Literally meaning "after this, therefore because of this," it deals with cause-and-effect relationships. It is the assumption that one event was the cause of the other, an assumption that is often difficult to support adequately.

Distorted example is another type of *non sequitur*. It is often used in deliberate efforts to deceive by means of an example that does not prove what it claims to prove. Thus, low grades supposedly prove that a student is inferior in an area. The distortion arises because other possibly important causes are ignored. The student may have been ill at the time of a major examination; or the test may have been deceptively worded, causing the use of a wrong approach.

Ignored effect is a type of fallacy that occurs when the author does not consider the consequences of a proposed course of action, which might cause more damage than the problem has caused.

Red herring is an argument that diverts attention from the central issue. Senator Joseph McCarthy was accused of using communism as a red herring for want of a better way to gain national attention. This is akin to the straw-man device that swells on minor, easily refuted points in order to avoid confronting the main issue.

Circular argument is often difficult to recognize since it uses itself to prove itself. Thus, a writer might support the claim that the Bible was written by God by citing quotations from the Bible. It is one form of the next fallacy, *begging the question.*

Begging the question is a device by which the speaker or author asks us to accept a contention on a basis other than evidence. The truth of the argument is assumed without proof. For example, an argument might be made that intelligent and informed people know smoking is hazardous to their health. The author, knowing that most people wish to be considered "intelligent and well informed," asks them to accept the contention as true without the support of solid evidence, such as medical studies.

Such faulty reasoning devices can destroy the case of any author, no matter that the conclusion is provable in other ways. It is the responsibility of the student to be able to recognize these common logical fallacies.

Writing the Report

The following outline will help the student produce an acceptable product.

    1. Identify the work. Use proper bibliographical citation form:

Book: Pescatello, Ann, ed. *Female and Male in Latin America: Essays*. Pittsburgh: University of Pittsburgh Press, 1973.

Article: Lynn, Naomi B., and Flora, Cornelia. "Motherhood and Political Participation: The Changing Sense of Self." *Journal of Military and Political Sociology* 1 (Spring 1971): 91-103.

2. Classify the work, e.g., fiction, nonfiction, biography, general account, special account, monograph, periodical article, essay, proceedings, etc.

3. Identify the author(s). Give their background and qualifications for writing the work (unless obvious).

4. Outline the thesis (if any). What is the theme, special "message," or point? Why has the author written this book this way; what is the purpose?

5. Note the organization. List the topics covered, scope of the work (or the selection), period covered, subjects omitted, factors not taken into account that influence the quality of the work. Has the author provided adequate maps, illustrative materials, etc.?

6. Check out the sources. Where has the author found the information? What kinds of sources are used—original manuscripts, monographs, secondary sources, interviews, etc.? Do you consider them adequate?

7. Note the amount read. List pages and chapters read and/or scanned. (If you read the entire work, give the number of pages.)

8. Do a critical evaluation. In a page or two, indicate what stands out—your personal reaction to the body of the work.

6

Scope and Biases of Newspapers, Columnists, and Commentators

Ideally, newspapers should be objective. That is, they should record what has happened with no hint of bias, no heavy hand of opinion. But such pristine purity is a myth. E. B. White, most sensitive of modern U. S. humor writers, has said that he who puts pen to paper writes, unavoidably, of himself. Reporters and columnists are people and as such have feelings and convictions that cannot be squeezed to death on the keyboard of the typewriter.

But even if such biases could be dealt with by the individual writer, hundreds of other aspects enter to blur the clean lines of objectivity. The length an editor allows the story to run, for instance, is a form of editorializing. So is the size of the headline placed above the story—and on the particular page itself. The fact that the story was printed and not discarded is the strongest and most obvious form of editorializing, since it calls for a basic opinion from the editor.

To cope with these conscious and subconscious biases, then, one must become aware of the general editorial tone of the publication he is reading.

One newspaper will bend over backwards to play a sensational rape-murder case on page one, while another will discard the story entirely. Others have pet projects or peeves that they continually overplay in their delight or pique; still others show an identifying lack of news judgment and a willingness to be guided in their story selection by the daily wire service log and outside publications.

Another point to be considered is the lack of real competition among newspapers today. Some 11,200 newspapers are published in the United States; about 1,800 are dailies.

Our population more than doubled during 1910-1970, but the number of dailies dropped by more than one third due to the economics of change forced by radio and TV. Today many states have not a single city with competing daily newspapers. In fact, daily newspaper competition survives in less than sixty of our cities.

These warnings are given in hope that the student will become a more critical and discerning reader.

Certain newspapers, like certain wines, are better or of a higher quality than others. This is due to a number of reasons—they emphasize political, economic, and cultural news; they are well written and have technical excellence; they have a tradition of freedom and economic independence; they have a strong editorial page and enterprising staff. In sum, they give careful in-depth coverage of significant events.

Among the top newspapers in the United States, those that have built over the years a reputation for excellent journalism are the *New York Times, Los Angeles Times, Christian Science Monitor, Washington Post, Wall Street Journal*, and *St. Louis Post-Dispatch.*

A large number of small-town newspapers, too, have extremely good reputations—they are, ironically, pressured in many ways into being good newspapers precisely because they are in small towns. No reporter or small-city editor can publish anything without being certain that someone will react directly, face-to-face. For this reason, when the small-city reporter gets the facts wrong, almost everybody in town knows it; they know the people involved, and they probably know of the incident reported.

The big-city reporter does not have this over-the-shoulder check on his or her work—and, it might be said, is the worse for it.

In May, 1970, a consensus of the American Newspaper Publishers Association decided that, in small towns where an editor has no anonymity, there is so much rapport between the newspaper and the reader that no one can get away with much. Great metropolitan dailies, on the other hand, can generalize and pervert the news to their own views, and often do, to the utter disregard of truth and fact.

As for their political biases, independently owned newspapers have a right, a duty even, to endorse on editorial pages those running for public office whom they favor and to crusade for or against any issue that so stirs them. Most daily newspapers, for instance, endorse a presidential candidate or a party ticket during an election campaign.

Table 6 shows how the American dailies shaped up politically during presidential campaigns in recent years, and Table 7 gives the state-by-state lineup of dailies for the 1972 presidential election.

At the same time, 23.3 percent of the responding papers, accounting for 14.9 percent of the circulation, declared they would remain uncommitted.

The results listed here are based on ballots from 1,054 dailies representing 59.8 percent of the 1,764 existing dailies listed in the *Editor & Publisher International Yearbook* for 1972. Their circulation totals 39,469,617 or 63.4 percent of the total daily U.S. circulation of 62,231,258.

The final compilation showed:

753 dailies with 30,560,535 circulation for Nixon
56 dailies with 3,044,534 circulation for McGovern
245 dailies with 5,864,548 circulation uncommitted

MAJOR POLITICAL COLUMNISTS

In twenty years, the events of the present will have been digested, analyzed, interpreted, and reinterpreted by a host of writers and academicians. But one need not always wait until

TABLE 6 / Editorial Endorsement of Presidential Candidates by United States Daily Newspapers

	% Papers	% Circulation
1944		
Dewey	60	68.5
Roosevelt	22	17.7
Uncommitted	18	13.8
1948		
Dewey	65	78.5
Truman	15	10
Others	4	1.5
Uncommitted	16	10
1952		
Eisenhower	67	80
Stevenson	14.5	11
Uncommitted	18.5	9
1956		
Eisenhower	63	72
Stevenson	15	13
Uncommitted	23	15
1960		
Nixon	57.7	70.9
Kennedy	16.4	15.8
Uncommitted	25.9	13.3
1964		
Goldwater	34.7	20.5
Johnson	42.4	62
Uncommitted	22.9	17.5
1968		
Nixon	60.8	69.9
Humphrey	14	19.3
Wallace	1.2	.3
Uncommitted	24	10.5
1972		
Nixon	71.4	77.4
McGovern	5.3	7.7
Uncommitted	23.3	14.9

Source: *Editor & Publisher*, Newspaper Trade Journal, November 5, 1960; October 31, 1964; November 2, 1968; November 4, 1972.

TABLE 7 / State-by-State Lineup of Dailies

	Nixon		McGovern		Independent or Uncommitted	
	No. of Papers	Circulation	No. of Papers	Circulation	No. of Papers	Circulation
Alabama	13	557,756	1	25,000	3	58,500
Alaska	2	17,550	–	–	2	19,300
Arizona	7	370,231	–	–	–	–
Arkansas	4	20,752	2	118,791	8	59,021
California	71	2,673,908	1	10,500	13	236,719
Colorado	15	635,650	1	3,500	2	72,000
Connecticut	8	324,152	1	12,000	8	261,520
Delaware	–	–	1	21,000	–	–
District of Columbia	1	415,884	–	–	–	–
Florida	26	1,447,545	2	68,027	–	79,400
Georgia	15	701,622	–	–	2	20,306
Hawaii	–	–	–	–	–	–
Idaho	4	56,086	1	3,850	2	11,050
Illinois	39	1,928,554	–	–	11	218,433
Indiana	39	1,059,250	4	46,674	10	82,885
Iowa	16	481,774	2	25,000	10	98,829
Kansas	32	330,725	1	53,000	8	245,026
Kentucky	10	170,732	2	262,304	4	31,043
Louisiana	8	212,167	–	–	6	170,510
Maine	4	181,000	1	10,529	1	24,000
Maryland	8	474,240	–	–	1	20,000
Massachusetts	13	712,828	2	19,200	9	221,179
Michigan	26	1,230,691	–	–	6	163,988
Minnesota	14	425,763	1	17,000	2	36,800
Mississippi	9	96,670	1	17,000	2	43,600
Missouri	23	1,511,755	3	21,747	9	86,894
Montana	7	94,456	–	–	3	76,500
Nebraska	9	130,760	–	–	3	32,500
Nevada	3	124,382	–	–	2	26,500
New Hampshire	3	95,172	1	11,000	2	26,000
New Jersey	15	992,049	3	256,500	–	–
New Mexico	10	88,379	–	–	4	31,200

TABLE 7 / Continued

	Nixon		McGovern		Independent or Uncommitted	
	No. of Papers	Circulation	No. of Papers	Circulation	No. of Papers	Circulation
New York	30	2,998,944	5	1,501,393	7	1,827,550
North Carolina	12	203,233	–	–	12	182,100
North Dakota	8	178,878	1	10,000	–	–
Ohio	40	2,503,860	1	4,000	12	203,144
Oklahoma	18	533,625	1	3,700	9	56,235
Oregon	9	95,153	2	146,500	4	79,500
Pennsylvania	40	1,180,541	3	93,500	17	388,158
Rhode Island	3	222,498	–	–	–	–
South Carolina	4	170,000	–	–	3	33,910
South Dakota	4	48,316	1	17,000	1	3,950
Tennessee	16	774,066	1	62,466	3	28,100
Texas	48	2,161,684	1	6,150	21	301,193
Utah	2	29,400	–	–	2	130,490
Vermont	4	63,477	2	14,200	2	29,500
Virginia	21	691,546	–	–	–	–
Washington	13	588,317	–	–	2	33,300
West Virginia	11	214,203	2	16,302	3	13,153
Wisconsin	13	294,729	2	82,000	4	74,000
Wyoming	3	45,579	2	16,302	3	13,153
Total	753	30,560,532	55	2,976,135	238	5,851,139
% of Total	72%	77.6%	5.2%	7.6%	22.7%	14.8%

news is history in order to place it in an intelligent perspective. This is the job of the political columnist. Every American newspaper worth its salt features several of these writer-scholars who try—with varying degrees of success—to make some kind of sense out of the events of each day. Their writing may differ—sheathed in humor or deadly logic, loaded with allegory or stripped down to the truth—but the target is the same: the current human condition and the reasons behind it.

Besides a strong individual writing style, the top news columnist brings to the job a predictable bias (political and ideological) and an individual standard of relevance that determines the type of news selected to focus on. Each columnist, regardless of political bias, has an individual sense of what is relevant, an individual focus on the news. For Tom Wicker, it is the burning social issue; for Jack Anderson, it is the behind-the-scenes exposé; for William Buckley, it is defense of the Right. This is subjective, point-of-view journalism, and the political points of view are many, as the following sketches show.

Jack Anderson

For more than twenty-five years, Jack Anderson and Drew Pearson wrote the daily column "The Washington Merry-Go-Round," which was syndicated in more than six hundred newspapers across the country. After Pearson's death (in 1969) Anderson has continued alone until 1975. He is now assisted by Les Whitten, an extremely intelligent young man who has taught at the college level, written a number of books, and worked as a reporter for the *Washington Post*.

The column has exposed more wrongdoing leading to actual court convictions or formal censure than all other Washington columnists' efforts combined. It was the columns of Pearson-Anderson that brought the focus of public opinion—and eventually the eye of the courts—on General Harry Vaughn in the Truman administration; on Sherman Adams and Bernard Goldfine in the Eisenhower administration; and on Bobby Baker, Adam Clayton Powell, and Thomas Dodd in the Johnson administration.

Although the column has attacked corruption in both parties and in individuals of all ideologies, its causes tend to be liberal ones: removal of the oil depletion allowance, regulation of highway billboards, promotion of the United Nations, and support of civil rights legislation.

More recently—in three short months in 1972—Anderson published: 1) secret papers showing a strong anti-India bias in the Nixon administration's handling of the India-Pakistan war (a Pulitzer Prize-winning effort); 2) the story of a U.S. ambassador getting drunk on a commercial airliner; 3) a report that the Justice Department had settled an antitrust suit against ITT on terms relatively favorable to the firm, about the same time that ITT had promised a contribution to the Republican convention fund.

Because Anderson has only a small paid staff, he uses his column to lure inside information, much of it being technically unsolicited. In this way, the column's notoriety works to his advantage. Many reporters who want to see a particular news story in print—a story that their own newspapers would not risk printing—will often turn it over to Anderson.

"The Washington Merry-Go-Round" is published daily by Anderson's home newspaper, the *Washington Post*—on the comics page.

Russell Baker

Armed with an unfailing sense of humor, *New York Times* syndicated columnist Russell Baker roams the countryside in search of windmills. When he finds one worthy of his lance, he quickly selects its weakest point and lunges.

His columns are heavily laced with satire with which he bastes the flesh of even the most sacred cows. As unbelievable as some of his material seems, it usually comes very close to some embarrassing truth. What Baker attempts to do is vary the pace of his column, to "sometimes. . .[be] in high dudgeon, sometimes . . . carry on a casual, convivial conversation with my readers."

He wrote the biographical note for the jacket of his recent book, *Poor Russell's Almanac*, with the same style and doubletake wit that mark his columns. "Russell Baker was born in 1853," he wrote, "aboard a schooner in the Malay Straits, served as a bagman for the railroad during the administration of Ulysses S. Grant, and graduated eight years later from the University of Heidelberg. . . .Mr. Baker holds many leading prizes and has made a fool of himself on many distinguished occasions. He has been dead for a number of years and has two cats."

This columnist's wanderings between fact and fiction leave a provocative trail; usually his fiction is more real than the news on page one. For instance, Russell Baker lives.

Jimmy Breslin

Formerly a columnist for the *New York Post*, the author of a novel, *The Gang That Couldn't Shoot Straight*, and from time to time a contributor to the weekly *New York Magazine*, Breslin these days is a kind of itinerant journalist.

Wherever his pieces appear, they are involved with the emotional impact of an issue rather than with the issue itself. When he was writing for the *Post*, he invented Runyonesque characters like Marvin the Torch and Fat Thomas to illustrate the absurdities of life in the city. Now he applies his personal approach to national issues and, not unlike Art Buchwald, has captured a fair-sized fan club of intellectuals. Of course, he gained a good bit of national exposure in 1969 when he joined author Norman Mailer for a brief plunge into New York City politics. They were beaten at the polls, but they cut a wide and memorable swath.

In June, 1975, he turned up as the first member of the *Washington Star-News* "writer-in-residence" program (the *Star* invites big name writers to town for an undetermined stint as columnists). His pieces did wonders for the morale of the regulars on the struggling *Star* as he vignetted such front-page impressions as an unnamed bureaucrat's futile attempt to seduce one of Breslin's co-workers.

"The *Star*," he told *Time*, "is the only place I could write in D.C.; the *Post* is too big and successful, like an insurance company."

A few years ago he visited Vietnam with the *New York Times* writer and editor James Reston. While Reston was talking to diplomats and generals, Breslin was interviewing foot soldiers. "Lodge and Rush and those people are not my set," he explained later. "I regard the whole scene like the 16th precinct in Manhattan. I don't get involved with anybody but the arresting officer and the desk sergeant."

Breslin has been called an anachronism, a man reporting in a style that went out with the speakeasy. True, perhaps, but his style of human, face-to-face reporting continues to draw readers across the country.

David Broder

Writing from a home base with the *Washington Post* syndicate, Broder has quietly built a solid reputation, bolstered in 1972 when he was voted the most respected political writer in the nation by fellow news reporters and again in 1973 when he was awarded a Pulitzer Prize for the consistent high quality of his political commentary.

Broder is difficult to classify for he tends to fall comfortably between the academic political scientist writing about political systems and the reporter-columnist writing about personalities and events. He does this by covering topics that are usually ignored by both textbooks and newspapers— areas such as the national party apparatuses, local party leaders, campaign organizations, and the complexities of the national convention.

But the most important feature of his columns is analysis. As do most political scientists, he views politics as a system; unlike most academicians, however, he has a weekly column in which to air his thoughts about that system.

"If I have a strong conviction about national politics," Broder has been quoted as saying, "it is that it's essentially local politics. The pros at [the national conventions] think first and foremost of the effect back home of decisions made at the convention."

Art Buchwald

Nothing is sacred to Buchwald, whose column, "Capitol Punishment," is the most widely syndicated humor column in the world (printed even in *Pravda* and *Izvestia*, Russia's leading daily newspapers). His technique is to take a complex situation and, by playing the role of a very naive analyst, reduce the issue to its logical absurdity. For example, in the midst of a column on the "Dirty Tricks Department" operated by the 1972 Committee to Re-elect the President, one of the Buchwald characters suggests darkly that the committee had even gone so far as to hire the opposing presidential candidate, George McGovern, and have him make major campaign blunders that would widen Nixon's margin of victory. "After all," he says, "he [McGovern] *is* short of cash."

Buchwald provides more than mere comic relief; his columns are sharply pointed and often deeply revealing as well.

William Buckley, Jr.

William Buckley brings a finely honed style, verve, humor, and a serious intellect to conservative political commentary. His column, "On the Right," is unique. His views are predictable: opposition to most government welfare programs, to federal support of racial integration, to the United Nations; support of just about all that is right of the political center, including his brother, Senator James Buckley of New York.

Oddly enough, an almost involuntary reaction finds him vigorously defending the latest public scapegoat who is being raked over the coals by other columnists. He once went so far as to defend the late Lyndon Johnson when the wolves were snapping at the Democratic ex-President's heels after publication of the Pentagon Papers. Thus, some of Buckley's views are not easily reconcilable with conventional conservatism, for he is a philosophical conservative (at time, indeed, a libertarian) who makes no pretense of practicality. He opposes snooping census takers, will consider the negative income tax, has expressed some sympathy for ghetto control of local schools, and denounces Robert Welch of the John Birch Society.

Buckley is at his best when fighting liberals with their own weapons—quotations from Thomas Jefferson, analogy, classical allusions, and devastating wit. When John Kenneth Galbraith appeared on a picket line of striking telephone employees to demonstrate his support, Buckley commented, "It was a nostalgic demonstration of an old faith, rather as if Marlene

Dietrich, emulating the Victorian ladies of yesteryear, were to faint upon hearing an obscenity."

It does not do to cross verbal swords with Buckley. He has always done his homework.

Marquis Childs

Marquis Childs writes full-length essays that appear as newspaper columns, and they are distinguished by their completeness. Unlike the newer style of columns, which emphasize only opinions, Childs does not take his readers' backgrounds for granted. When he evaluated Hubert Humphrey's chances in Michigan in 1968, for example, his column was typically 35 percent longer than most, and it was also a short course in Michigan politics.

This thorough approach is understandable, for Childs is also an established author with several best sellers to his credit. In the early 1930s he attended a housing conference in Scandinavia and became so interested in the Swedish experiment in non-Marxist socialism that he wrote the best seller *Sweden: The Middle Way* (New Haven, Conn.: Yale University Press, 1936). Since then, he has written a number of other books, including *Eisenhower: Captive Hero* (New York: Harcourt Brace Jovanovich, 1958), and several political novels, the latest being *Taint of Conscience* (New York: Harper & Row, 1967), about international spying.

Childs's liberal orientation goes back to Franklin Roosevelt and the New Deal. Despite his long identification with liberal causes, he is not an insider to the "liberal establishment." His idealism has in the past kept him from the inner circle, for John F. Kennedy was friendly to tough-minded Joseph Alsop and Lyndon Johnson confided in elite-oriented William S. White. Childs has supported liberal Democratic goals since the early 1930s, but he has never accepted the bargaining and deals that politicians feel are necessary to accomplish them. His columns and his books have an idealistic and independent tinge. Frequently, he tends to write somewhat "off the news," discussing a threat to privacy or civil liberties while a world crisis is dominating the headlines.

Rowland Evans and Robert Novak

In a revealing interview published by the magazine *Potomac*, these political journalists described their column as reportage rather than interpretation. Novak said:

> I really think editors are surfeited with armchair opinion and are crying for reasonably accurate, factual reporting on politics. What we are really trying to do is intersect the lines of communication in Washington. Anyone who has enough energy can do it. . . . We just sort of scramble. It makes people feel they know what is going on inside. We take a strong point of view on a situation, but we're not strongly doctrinaire. Neither Rowly nor I is terribly profound. I don't think we're in business to point up the good; we're trying to show the foibles of people. The conservatives claim that we're a liberal column and the liberals claim we're a conservative column, which I think shows that we're doing a good job of stepping on a lot of toes.

Evans further commented, "We think there's a conflict everywhere, and our job is to find it and reveal it. And I know damned well there's conflict in heaven." In the decade or so since their column originated, Evans and Novak have exposed a good deal of conflict.

Many of their columns are devoted to the machinery of organized politics. They were the first to describe Richard Nixon's well developed national organization for capturing the Republican nomination (in 1968), and they later broke the first big story of the Nixon administration by revealing several days before the formal announcement that Melvin Laird was to be Secretary of Defense. In 1975, their column took readers into a White House congressional breakfast on foreign policy. Supporting Henry Kissinger against attacks by Congress, the columnists wrote: "In a dangerous world with Western power declining and Soviet power gaining, how can the U.S. deal with the Soviet Union at the same time a leaderless Congress is running wild with its own foreign policy dictated by the pressures of domestic politics?"

Art Hoppe

This San Francisco humor columnist, not always happy with the world as it is reported in the rest of the newspaper, has succeeded in creating one of his own. Hoppe's world is really no better than the real world, but in it selfishness, stupidity, and hypocrisy are easier to identify.

Hoppe uses all the common weapons in a humorist's arsenal, exaggeration, pathos, and logical absurdity, to explode the pomposity of the world as he sees it. He employs these weapons in a continuing series of fables, parables, and mythical organizations. One of his columns begins:

> One of the most burning moral issues of our time is capital punishment. And after carefully weighing the arguments on both sides, I'd like to say a few words about the death penalty: It isn't enough. The purpose of the death penalty, everybody agrees, is to show killers that killing people is bad. Which we do by killing them. And that sure shows them. But is this example effective on potential killers? Not very. Because no matter how many people we kill to show people that killing people is bad, people still go on killing people. Obviously then, the death penalty alone isn't a strong enough deterrent. And after much thought, I have formed the Bring Back the Rack Committee, a do-good organization.

Hoppe's bias is generally liberal, and like many social critics, he can be quite self-righteous. His nationally syndicated column, however, is quite enjoyable, and it brings to light the ultimate absurdity of many American policies.

Murray Kempton

Journalist and author, Murray Kempton was a columnist for seventeen years with the *New York Post*, before becoming a freelance writer in 1969. He tends to focus upon personalities in the news. His writing style can be characterized as compact, terse, allusive, and, at times, haunting. *Harper's Magazine* once observed: "Mr. Kempton has a nice sense of how much effort to give to the daily column; he throws himself away and blows material in a paragraph that his more economic competitors would stretch into a ten-part series." Says Democratic Congressman Richard Bolling of Missouri of Kempton (*Newsweek*, June 17, 1963): "Sometimes I can't understand what he's saying, but the end effect is enormous. He's a breath of fresh air with political insights."

Kempton has also been known for crusading articles. During the McCarthy era, he spoke out publicly to defend the civil liberties of Communists; in 1961, he participated in civil rights freedom marches in the South. And in 1968, he actively supported Senator Eugene McCarthy for president. That same year, he joined antiwar protesters in Washington and was arrested and fined for disorderly conduct. His latest work has included news commentaries on CBS radio's *Spectrum* series and a book on the Black Panthers and the quality of American justice.

James Kilpatrick

For many years James Kilpatrick was the Old South's most literate and articulate defender of racial segregation. His editorials in the *Richmond News Leader* led to national prominence and, eventually, to a television debate with Martin Luther King, Jr.

Kilpatrick defended segregation from the position of an elite conservative—one who valued the genteel life of "the good old days" as he remembered them and who did not want to see them changed.

Today Kilpatrick's column has changed, and segregation is no longer a topic. Still, his innate conservatism serves as a useful basis for a general political column. Kilpatrick has a crisp, elegant style, and when he finds stupidity and mismanagement in the world around him, he attacks it with real force. Like William Buckley, he also defends those under attack by the liberal establishment, all of which is the classic suit of the conservative. And it fits Kilpatrick. This is not to arbitrarily denigrate the conservative role in American politics, for politicians have a saying that it takes a liberal to carry out a reactionary policy and a conservative to push a progressive one.

Joseph Kraft

Kraft, who was a Phi Beta Kappa at Columbia University and spent a year at Princeton's Institute for Advanced Study, writes a thoughtful, philosophical column stressing the complexity of political problems and the necessity for more than common sense and clear thinking to solve them. He is the journalistic link to the new breed of "policy intellectuals" who are playing a growing role in governmental decision making.

His column on the national defense budget heaped praise on Secretary of Defense James Schlesinger for a "realistic approach":

> The most striking feature of the positive statement (presented to Congress the other day, increasing defense spending from $85 to $93 billion) is the absence of blarney. Gone are the blowhard rhetoric about Communist intentions and the tricky accounting which made supplemental budgetary requests inevitable. . . . So it is now up to the Congress to discipline itself—to handle the defense budget in a way that complements the responsible and honest case made by probably the best strategist we ever had in the Pentagon.

Kraft generally supports liberal goals (he was a speech writer for John Kennedy) but refuses to be classified as a liberal. In fact, while supporting the goals of Kennedy and Johnson, he was also quite critical of their "shortsightedness" in meeting those goals. Kraft is one of the first writers to bring to a newspaper column the resources of policy-oriented intellectuals—an approach that will become more and more important in a "postindustrial" society in which the university is the dominant institution.

David Lawrence

Lawrence, who died in 1973, literally invented the syndicated political columnist, having written his Washington column since 1916. He was the acknowledged dean of Washington correspondents. For three generations he was the unquestioned voice of conventional conservatism. When looking back over his work, it is important to remember that he was the publisher of *U.S. News & World Report* and was, therefore, likely to maintain the conservative line in all areas of policy. His columns generally fell neatly into two categories—exposition and opinion. On the strength of his many years spent observing the Washington scene, Lawrence was able to make the subtlest of political comparisons, such as that between James Cox's fate as heir to a failing Wilson administration in 1920 and Hubert Humphrey's plight in 1968. His longevity gave him an instinct for the voter's feelings that was seldom matched by professional pollsters.

Generally, Lawrence was as predictable as the planets. His policy position was very near that of the more conservative Republicans and Southern Democrats. Thus, he supported the war in Vietnam, opposed foreign aid and other foreign entanglements, suspected most domestic spending programs, and deplored the most recent Supreme Court decisions of his day. One of his last magazine columns before his death praised America's involvement in Vietnam and agreed with Nixon that we had "attained peace with honor."

Walter Lippmann

For many years Walter Lippmann's column, "Today and Tomorrow," provided a perspective of history in the form of journalism of today. It is difficult to describe the full impact of this man on American political leaders. When he died in December 1974 at the age of eighty-five, he left unfinished the manuscript of his twenty-seventh book. Even in his last days he continued to speak out. He praised Nixon's diplomatic moves toward China and the Soviet Union, but he criticized the Watergate crisis as "the worst scandal in our history."

James Reston, himself a respected reporter and columnist, pointed out that when Lippmann returned from a trip to Russia and Germany "his reports were part of the common conversation of the Capitol. Every embassy up and down Sixteenth Street and Massachusetts Avenue discussed them and reported them to their governments. Members of the Senate Foreign Relations Committee read them and questioned the Secretary of State on his points."

Walter Lippmann seemed able to interpret the intentions of American policy better than can the official policymakers themselves. Patrick O'Donovan of the *London Observer* wrote, "State Department officials answering general questions in private quite often say 'Have you read Lippmann on that?' "

Lippmann earned this praise and influence in a journalistic career that began under the tutelage of Lincoln Steffens in 1912. In the decades that followed, Lippmann wrote a number of books, many of which are required reading in college courses today: *Public Opinion* (New York: Crowell-Collier and Macmillan, 1922); *Preface to Politics* (New York: Crowell-Collier and Macmillan, 1933); *Essays in the Public Philosophy* (Boston: Little, Brown, 1955); *Drift and Mastery* (Englewood Cliffs, N.J.: Prentice-Hall, 1961), to name but a few.

Lippmann had such influence because he was an original political thinker. In his own words, he "lived two lives," one of philosophy that provided the context of his day-to-day observation of people and events, and one of journalism that provided the "laboratory" in which to test the philosopy and keep it from becoming too abstract. As a political thinker he grappled with such fundamental political issues as elite leadership in a democracy, the formulation of issues, the relevance of liberal democracy in the twentieth century, natural law, the limitations of public opinion, and isolationism.

It is impossible to place Lippmann on the usual political spectrum, for he endorsed Republicans and Democrats and was conservative on one issue and liberal on another. Yet, he remained so singularly judicious that he neither offended nor enraged his opponents. In his careful weighing and balancing of factors that shaped the great issues, he was rarely entirely satisfactory to partisans of either side. On the most important issue of the late 1960s, the Vietnam war, he was an early opponent of American policy and reluctantly endorsed Richard Nixon as the best hope of withdrawal.

For over forty years Lippmann's columns, first in the *New York World* and later in the *New York Herald Tribune,* provided the intellectual agenda for those who wished to understand public policy. In his last years his columns appeared only fortnightly in *Newsweek* magazine.

Time magazine's eulogy to Walter Lippmann stated:

> He could have held his own in an 18th-century salon or coffeehouse, sparring civilly with the prophets of the Enlightenment. . . . His prowess at drawing history's sweep from the minutiae of daily events might have impressed even Gibbon. Had they discoursed on politics, he and Edmund Burke would have found themselves on the same aloof Olympian plane.

Anthony Lewis

In recent years, Lewis, from his position as head of the *New York Times* London bureau, has fashioned a brilliant string of news exclusives. Earlier, as a Nieman Fellow concentrating on the Supreme Court, he wrote *Gideon's Trumpet,* perhaps the most readable and perceptive book on the U.S. legal system ever written for the layman.

Since 1969 he has been writing a twice-a-week column from London, which means that twice a week he attempts to make the difficult transition from the traditionally dispassionate reporter to what has been called "the emotional commitment indispensable to a columnist."

His column has evoked a good deal of criticism from readers, who generally charge that London is not the proper base from which to comment on the United States. His editors, however, seem to feel that, on occasion, distance gives an important perspective. Lewis, himself, concedes that keeping his two roles separate takes a good deal of introspection and personal review. He is convinced, though, that he has done it.

Mary McGrory

Mary McGrory writes about the human factor behind behavior. "I have very few opinions," she once told an interviewer, "but powerful impressions." It was these impressions that won her a Pulitzer Prize in 1974 for her work on the Watergate story. Her style has been described as the "poet's gift of analogy," referring to the effect she creates by combining classical literary allusions with current feelings and events. And if one may call acid etchings poetry, the comment is valid.

Ms. McGrory gained national recognition with her descriptions of the Army-McCarthy hearings in the early 1950s, one of which painted Roy Cohen, Senator Joseph McCarthy's counsel, as "a boy who has had a letter sent home from school about him and has come back to his elders to get the whole thing straightened out."

She has a subtle and indirect influence on attitudes. Her writing reflects the feelings that most people have but cannot express. One of her more memorable I-wish-I'd-said-that's described a campaigning Richard Nixon: "He still stalks the light touch with all the grimness that butterfly collectors bring to the pursuit of a rare specimen."

Ms. McGrory writes in these hues for the *Washington Star-News,* which syndicates her column nationally.

James Reston

James (Scotty) Reston is perhaps America's most outstanding columnist. Elevated from the Washington bureau of the *New York Times,* he is now among the management team at the paper and would be hidden there were it not for his columns that emerge cloaked in stunning significance and perception. Mainly, he dwells on the likely and specific consequences of a given political action, discussing why a particular event occurred and what will happen as a result.

Reston was the acknowledged master of the art of extracting facts from officials by pretending to already know the whole story. Often, in fact, he did know the whole story, for the *New York Times* Washington bureau has for years been a formidable news-gathering machine.

It is important to note about this journalist that he not only reports and interprets the news, but that also he *influences* it. His is the journalism of involvement. (William Rivers, in his book, *The Opinion-Makers,* notes instances in presidential administrations going back to Franklin Roosevelt in which Reston directly or indirectly influenced political events.)

Reston has always been a political realist, respecting politicians who operate effectively while living up to their own ideals, and criticizing those who fall short.

Readers of his column may be certain that official Washington will be talking about his material that day—and that within a week other columnists will be addressing themselves to the same topic.

John Roche

Best known as an academician of liberal leaning, Roche began writing a nationally syndicated column in 1968. Until then, his credentials were mainly campus-colored: professor of politics at Brandeis University from 1956 to 1973; chairman of the Americans for Democratic Action; a former consultant to Hubert Humphrey and Lyndon Johnson; and a member of the executive committee of the American Political Science Association.

His books include works on American political thought as put forth by Jefferson and John Marshall. As of 1975, he was serving as a professor of civilization and foreign affairs at the Fletcher School of Law and Diplomacy in Medford, Massachusetts.

Several years ago Roche, in a major article, took to task the inside chroniclers of the U.S. presidency. As he saw it, the problem was that insiders like Sorenson, Schlesinger, and Reedy knew both too much and not enough. "They knew what was happening . . . but they simply could not document what actually happened."

Roche doubts that an accurate appraisal of the Kennedy and Johnson years can be written within the next twenty years. Enough time must be allowed to pass, he has said, to allow the immediate lines to bend toward perspective.

William Safire

When Safire was hired away from the Nixon administration by the *New York Times,* there were those who felt the great newspaper had gathered a viper to its fold. After all, he was the President's man; and both the President and Vice-President Agnew had blazed a political trail of antimedia words and actions.

But Safire took to his new desk like a king's envoy taking a room at the inn. "I have a point of view like the President's," he admitted, "but I'll call it the way I see it."

Counterbalancing the other *Times* columnists—Wicker, Reston, Lewis et al.—the new resident conservative rather consistently saw it the Nixon way, bringing forth columns in defense of his former boss's role in the Watergate affair. *Washington Post* columnist Nicholas Von Hoffman wrote that the *Times* "could have saved itself about 50 grand a year, if they just sent an office boy over to pick up the White House press releases."

Nixon is gone and Hoffman lost his job on the CBS television show *Sixty Minutes,* but Safire is still pecking away at the *Times,* calling it the way he sees it.

I. F. Stone

There is so much to say about Izzy Stone that it seems unfair to classify him simply as a newsman, a journalist. "Hell," he once told some students, "I was a news reporter when I was 14." He turned 68 in 1975.

He came to national attention through his newsletter, *I. F. Stone's Weekly,* which, from its beginnings in 1953 to its end in 1973, touched on every major issue of the day, full of its editor-writer's opinions and analyses and documented in a way that few newspapers or magazines document their stories today. Through the *Weekly* (which became *Bi-Weekly* in 1968), Stone was the first to touch on many of the "untouchable" issues of his day: McCarthy and the witchhunt, the race battle, poverty, democracy, and other sacred cows. He folded his publishing tent in 1973 to join the *New York Review of Books* as its political columnist.

A sketch in the *Columbia Journalism Review* described him as ". . . a whole political man, a remarkable integration of courage, persistency, unintimidatable honesty, learning, curiosity, modesty, humor. A dissenter always, he has never played the cynic." Stone has described himself as a "combination of maniacal zest and idiot zeal—a newspaperman."

Cyrus Leo Sulzberger

New York Times columnist Cy Sulzberger has been covering international events for more than thirty years. His experiences as chief of the *New York Times* foreign correspondents have given him a well-defined philosophy of the world, which he has never been hesitant to phrase: "Our business is neither ideological warfare nor the rigid maintenance of any status quo. Our business is to protect our own national interests from any threat, regardless of its philosophical label, and to try and see that changes in an ever-changing world are sufficiently controlled to avoid excessively dangerous explosions."

With the exception of his many columns on Vietnam, Sulzberger usually writes somewhat "off the news." He tries to bring particular events into a general framework and to prepare his readers for future flareups. Writing about the Czech crisis, for instance, he said that the real crisis was for the Russians. "Unless they can apply some of the changes pioneered in Czechoslovakia, the whole system will collapse."

Sulzberger and Joseph Alsop were the two major columnists defending the Vietnam war who could not be identified as conservatives. Sulzberger put Vietnam in world perspective—his own world perspective, to be sure—but it is still an overall view. The United States, he feels, has a continuing responsibility to live up to the role of world superpower, which it inherited in 1945.

Hunter Thompson

"Getting assigned to cover Nixon [is] like being sentenced to six months in a Holiday Inn." That's vintage Thompson, an off-beat, subterranean, far out, profane, and often just plain vicious political columnist for *Rolling Stone. Rolling Stone* is an underground, commercially successful biweekly circulating from San Francisco to around 300,000 readers.

Thompson has been called the counterculture's most listened to voice. His column is labeled "Fear and Loathing" and it scintillates. "In fact, it's the only stuff on this campaign I can bear to read." That was Nicholas Von Hoffman of the *Washington Post,* who is himself regarded suspiciously by the establishment press.

It has been said that everything that Thompson observes seems to buttress his conviction that the power structure is crawling with phonies. He once wrote, "Half the conversation on a press bus is about who lied to whom today, but nobody ever prints the fact that they're goddam liars."

Hunter Thompson is a stone fanatic on the subject of truth.

Nicholas Von Hoffman

For the last several years Nicholas Von Hoffman has written a column for and been syndicated by the *Washington Post.* The *Post* blandly calls it "Comment," but it is the vehicle for some of the most outrageous liberal slants on social and moral issues that the American public has ever been exposed to.

Von Hoffman writes with the white heat of a *Rolling Stone* crusader. His interests reek of beads and faded jeans; his prose, of dinner jackets and drawing rooms. He can bite with the most acerbic in the business and would be a perfect balance on the same editorial page with William Buckley: Von Hoffman on the left; Buckley on the right.

Arrogant, elegant, and suave, Von Hoffman strips away his subject's pretensions, slashing in controlled fury at industry, military, AMA, politicians, officious officials, and the sorry state of journalism.

He once described Judge Julius Hoffman, who sat for the Chicago Seven trial: " . . . the teeny judge, who bounces up and down on his bench so that he looks like a small girl in an oversized dress playing in her father's chair." Von Hoffman is a sandaled radical with the style of a dauphin.

William S. White

White admires men of power, but he does not favor dissenters, such as Senator Eugene McCarthy or Robert Kennedy. He writes about elite politics, focusing on the problem of inner-circle negotiations. His interest in political professionals has naturally made him a great admirer of Lyndon Johnson and, in fact, the title of his laudatory Johnson biography is *The Professional* (Boston: Houghton Mifflin, 1964).

His sympathy and understanding for the problems of powerful leaders have paid off in access and friendships that have crossed party lines to include Robert Taft, Dwight Eisenhower, Lyndon Johnson, and Richard Nixon.

White has an ability to discover and write about those obscure facets of personality that allow one leader to develop a rapport with another. When he leaves the inner circle of elite politics, however, his power of analysis weakens and blinds him to the popular appeal exhibited at one time or another by such men as Robert Kennedy, William Fulbright, or Eugene McCarthy. He should be read for his exclusive access to and deep understanding of leaders—particularly with regard to ex-President Nixon—but his strong bias must be kept in mind.

Tom Wicker

Tom Wicker's special contribution as a columnist is his ability to identify problem situations before they emerge. He inherited the venerable Arthur Krock's "In the Nation" column on the editorial page of the *New York Times* and has given the column his own special emphasis.

Wicker travels widely, attempting to identify local situations that will have a national significance. In 1966 he attended a political rally in Pioneer Park, Wyoming, and described the crowd's reactions to national, state, and local candidates. In doing so he identified and brought to life many political science generalizations about campaigning that usually remain buried in textbooks. That same year he wrote a three-column series on the guaranteed annual income that was a thoroughly sophisticated, but understandable, exposition of a complex issue. Wicker's columns are more readable and exhibit greater force than the usual objective exposition, because he is not reluctant to take sides. He selected the annual income topic because he was favorably disposed toward the idea. In explaining his position, he related the proposal to ideas and values that were already familiar to his readers: "Guaranteed annual income is not something for nothing at all, but an idea that basically confirms the American reluctance to put people on the dole and the American belief in helping people to help themselves."

Wicker favors liberal causes—such as massive urban programs and civil rights. In recent years, he has willingly exchanged the role of impartial observer for that of participant. In 1971 he urged his readers to engage in civil disobedience in protesting against the war in Southeast Asia. "We got one President out," he wrote, "and perhaps we can do it again." Later the same year, inmates at Attica prison named Wicker to the Citizens' Mediating Committee to inspect prison conditions and observe talks between inmates and prison officials. And in

1972 he openly wrote of his admiration for Senator George S. McGovern, the Democratic candidate for president. Activist stands such as these have served to make the *New York Times* columnist more popular with the public than with his professional colleagues.

NATIONAL TELEVISION'S POLITICAL COMMENTATORS

David Brinkley

A native of Wilmington, N.C., the "other half" of the famous Huntley-Brinkley news team at NBC began his journalism career as a teenage reporter for the *Wilmington Star-News* in 1938. He joined NBC in 1943 and has been with that network ever since.

Since 1951 he has specialized in Washington politics, which he reported on so well that he was given the slot of co-anchorman—with the late Chet Huntley—on NBC's evening news program. Together, Huntley and Brinkley formed the most listened-to broadcast news team in the nation, outrating all competition.

Brinkley's wry Carolina wit and his ability to make concise assessments of complex issues have kept him popular with national viewers, even though, after Huntley's death, he resigned as the NBC anchorman and now provides political commentary instead. In his new role, he is seen less but has more freedom to select topics.

John Chancellor

In mid-August of 1971, for the first time in fifteen years, NBC went on the air with a single anchorman for its nightly news telecast. The man given the unenviable task of following the Huntley-Brinkley success was John Chancellor.

Thoughtful, urbane, quietly dignified, Chancellor brought to the evening news slot a ream of outstanding credentials. Starting as a newspaper copyboy, he worked as a writer for

NBC, a newsman on radio's *Monitor* program, emcee of the *Today* show, and, over the years, the head of five overseas news bureaus for NBC. He took leave from his network during 1965-67 to head the Voice of America operation.

Among his notable accomplishments are his coverage of the Arkansas school integration fight in 1957 and his reporting of five presidential election campaigns.

Walter Cronkite

Walter Cronkite is an American institution. In a recent poll taken by the Oliver Quayle organization, one question asked concerned the degree of trust placed in various public figures. The easy winner, with 73 percent of the vote, was the famed CBS news anchorman. Why? Columnist Jack Anderson says a good deal of it is image: "He comes across as a really sincere, believable guy. . . . He's a good, thorough newsman, very professional, very able." Nicholas Von Hoffman put it more succinctly: "Well, he's America's old shoe. He's the national security blanket. We just *love* him."

Cronkite's professional reputation rests on his rigid objectivity, which forces him to spend hours in preparation for a story. Preparation like that has brought him wide praise for his superior handling of scheduled events like the first lunar landing.

He began his career as a correspondent in World War II and was a radio performer as well as a reporter right from the beginning. He got his start in television in 1950 as a CBS correspondent in Washington, and he has been with that network since.

William Moyers

Propelled into the national spotlight as President Johnson's press secretary, Bill Moyers has since gone on to other, more subdued successes. He has served as publisher of *Newsday*, a Long Island daily newspaper, as an author, and as a news commentator seen weekly over the Public Broadcast System (PBS) outlets across the nation. *Newsweek* magazine has labeled the Moyer news-journal program "one of the most provocative public affairs programs since [Edward R.] Murrow."

Moyers writes, edits, and does most of the reporting for the show. On the air, he sees his job as "keeping the conversation going." Those he has interviewed have included Swedish economist Gunnar Myrdal and CBS's Walter Cronkite.

Harry Reasoner

Reasoner joined the CBS news department in 1956 and worked there until 1970 when he joined ABC as half of that network's one-two punch with Howard K. Smith.

Reasoner, born April 17, 1923, began his career as a journalist with the *Minneapolis Times* (now defunct) in 1942, was drafted into the army, and rejoined the *Times* in 1946. Two years later he was fired for writing an unfavorable review of a musical from New York. "It was one of those road shows from New York that came to Minneapolis," he once admitted in an interview, "and the theory was that you couldn't criticize them or they'd stop coming."

In 1948 he signed on with WCCO in Minneapolis, a CBS radio network affiliate and followed that stint three years later with a position with the U.S. Information Agency as writer and editor of its Far East operation and was stationed in Manila for the next three years. He went back to Minneapolis in 1954, working for KEYD-TV (now KMSP-TV) as news director until 1956 when the network beckoned him to New York City.

A *New York Times* columnist wrote that "Mr. Reasoner's chief contribution is to take the curse off the lifeless wire service prose of hourly newscasts. To items that already may have been broadcast several times, he imparts a turn of phrase that catches a listener's attention, and he is not hesitant in using . . . his own dry humor where warranted."

In 1970 he was lured to ABC as co-anchorman with Howard K. Smith, and finally, as lone anchorman after Smith was moved to be ABC's answer to Eric Sevareid of CBS.

In an interview by *TV Guide,* Reasoner compared covering the White House to a police beat, "except on a very high level."

His dry wit and reportorial objectivity have combined to raise him to the top of the heap among electronic news reporters, giving him the opportunity to display what has been called "a facile blend of irony and lucidity in his reporting, a talent for composing the broadcast essay on piquant side lines to the news."

Eric Sevareid

One of broadcast journalism's favorites, Eric Sevareid dazzled his constituents with more than three decades of news scoops, disarming wit, and accurate analyses. He was personally selected by the late Edward R. Murrow to join "Murrow's Boys," a group of top newspaper reporters gathered by Murrow to cover World War II. These handpicked reporters enabled CBS to dominate the radio news field for years to come. And Sevareid was a standout among the talent as he courageously made the last broadcast from Paris by an American, fleeing the city just before it was overrun by the German Army. It was shortly afterwards that he scored one of the best scoops in journalism history: He filed the first story to reveal that France was about to capitulate and sue for an armistice.

After the war CBS used him for a variety of assignments, but he made his name as one of the mainstays of CBS presidential election coverage teams.

Finally, in 1964, Eric Sevareid was appointed national correspondent for the network, which also made him a regular participant on *CBS Evening News* with Walter Cronkite. He appears these days mainly as the network's news analyst and as the program's editorial voice. His beautifully tailored two-or-three-minute essays have drawn praise from critics and from viewers. A *New York Times* reviewer, for instance, once wrote

of a CBS special narrated by Sevareid that the telecast
". . . performed the happy function of restoring [him] to
television at his perceptive and witty best. Mr. Sevareid always
has been one of the ablest essayists in broadcasting. . . . "

Sevareid has always referred to himself as a writer, not a
performer, and has described his political philosophy in recent
years as liberal on domestic affairs and "increasingly conservative" on foreign affairs.

Howard K. Smith

The other half of ABC's top news team of Reasoner-Smith,
Howard K. Smith joined the team in January of 1962 as
anchorman.

He brought to that network a list of journalistic credentials
that spanned World War II and a scholastic background that
jerked him to top-level attention in the medium.

Starting in 1939 he worked for United Press news wire
service in London, moved to Copenhagen and then, in the white
heat of Hitler's Nazism, to Berlin in 1940. The following year
he joined CBS's "Murrow's Boys," becoming a key part of a
team of reporters who dominated worldwide coverage for the
next decade. He wound up his overseas assignments with memorable coverage of the Nuremberg war criminal trials in 1946.

He returned to the United States that year as moderator,
commentator and/or reporter for such CBS programs as *Face
the Nation, Eyewitness to History, The Great Challenge,* and
numerous news specials. Finally in 1961 he was elevated to
chief correspondent and manager of the CBS Washington
Bureau, whence he was lured away by *ABC Evening News* as
anchorman.

Barbara Walters

Named a woman of the year by the *Ladies' Home Journal*
in 1974, Ms. Walters is the highest paid journalist in television,
better paid even than Walter Cronkite. The *Today* show, on

which she stars, has won two Emmy awards and is NBC's most lucrative daytime show—even though it is aired in the wee hours of the morning across the nation.

Despite her achievements, however, Barbara Walters is one of the most disliked personalities on American television. As a trailblazer in woman's television journalism, she has had to endure many criticisms that her male counterparts have not. When Mike Wallace, for instance, attacks an interview subject, he is generally admired for his aggressive, let-the-chips-fall-where-they-may style; when Ms. Walters does the same thing, she is most often seen as "pushy."

However "pushy" she might be, she is known among her fellow journalists for asking the toughest questions in the business. They may not sound tough, coated, as they so often are, in her throaty feminine tones, but her thorough preparation for interviews repeatedly shows up in her ". . . was it then that you stole the money, Senator" bombs.

The interview that stands out most vividly in her memory was one with Robert Kennedy, when the late Senator was campaigning in the 1968 presidential primaries. She recalls, "I'd heard all those stories about how cold and tough he was. And then we met; he seemed so young and boyish, and his hand shook under the desk as I interviewed him."

7

Statistics

Many of the articles and books used in political science employ statistical concepts and symbols. In order to judge these materials adequately the student must be able to evaluate the soundness of the methodology used. In addition, the student involved in research will be asking questions the answers to which must be found through the application of quantitative procedures. One of the strongest arguments for quantitative techniques is that one is forced to move away from individual judgment and personal bias toward more objective criteria. The following material is included only as a first step in acquainting the student with some of the most commonly used statistical procedures and terms.

Statistics is a technique that uses scientific procedures for collecting, organizing, analyzing, and presenting numerical data. *Descriptive statistics* is used to describe a collection of quantitative information in a form that is more concise and convenient than the raw data. Its primary purpose is thus to summarize research data. *Statistical inference* is basically the act of drawing conclusions from the data. It permits the investigator to generalize about a large group called the *population*, which cannot be observed, from a representative portion of the group called a *sample*. Both description and inference are utilized in most statistical studies. Knowledge of the two techniques makes it possible for students to read publications intelligently and to develop the skills required to do their own research.

The basic level of classification is *nominal.* This involves sorting elements into categories. These categories should be exhaustive and mutually exclusive. Ranking such categories with respect to the magnitude of qualities to be compared results in an *ordinal scale.* Ordinal scales allow quantities to be ranked according to size or amount, but they do not give a specific mathematical measure of the difference between categories. When one can not only rank categories in order of magnitude but also determine exactly how much more or less each group has than other groups, he or she is working with an *interval scale.* Knowing which (nominal, ordinal, or interval) level of measurement can legitimately be used with the data is the first step in determining the appropriate statistical technique to be used.

DESCRIPTIVE STATISTICS

The *central tendency* of a distribution is a single typical or representative score that describes the whole group. The two most important measures of central tendency are the *mean* and the *median.* The *mean* is what is usually called the average. It is the sum of the scores divided by the total number of cases involved. The mean is usually represented by the uppercase M or by $\overline{X}$. The formula for the arithmetic mean is $\overline{X} \text{ (or M)} = \dfrac{\Sigma X}{N}$ where

$\overline{X}$ (or M) = arithmetic mean
Σ = sum of
X = the value of items in the collection
N = number of items

The *median* is the value of the middle item when the scores are arranged according to size.

The *mode* is another measure of central tendency and refers to the category that occurs most frequently. In selecting a measure of central tendency, the level of measurement available is the primary consideration. If you are using nominal data only, the mode can be used. With ordinal data the mode or median can be used. With interval data the mode, median, or mean can be used.

Tables 8, 9, and 10 illustrate these three measures with elementary examples. One point shown here is usually encountered: the mean of a series is usually above the median because larger values exert a strong effect on the mean and pull it up.

TABLE 8 / Wages Per Hour of Women Working in the Duston City Library

$1.75
1.75
2.20
2.00
1.90

TABLE 9 / Wages in Table 8 Arranged in Numerical Order As an *Array*

$1.75
1.75
1.90
2.00
2.20

TABLE 10 / Arithmetic Mean of Data in Table 9

$$
\begin{array}{r}
\$1.75 \\
1.75 \\
1.90 \\
2.00 \\
\underline{2.25} \\
9.65
\end{array}
$$

$$\overline{X} = \frac{\Sigma X}{N} = \frac{9.65}{5} = \$1.93$$

Median and Mode

$$
\begin{array}{l}
\$1.75 \quad \text{Mode} \\
1.75 \\
1.90 - \text{Median*} \\
2.00 \\
2.25
\end{array}
$$

. . . .

*For an even numbered series, take a value halfway between the two items nearest the middle:

$$
\begin{array}{l}
\$1.60 \\
1.70 \\
\qquad \text{Median is \$1.75} \\
1.80 \\
1.90
\end{array}
$$

MEASURES OF DISPERSION

Social scientists are interested not only in characterizing measurements by central or average values, but they also want to know how closely the measurements are bunched together or how much each unit deviates from the mean. For example, are most women in certain occupations close to the average age or is there a wide spread of ages with not many falling into the average age category? The extent of dispersion or variability of the group will be of special interest to the behavioral scientist.

The simplest measure of dispersion is the *range*. The *range* includes the upper and lower limits of all the observations made. If, from the membership rolls of the League of Women Voters we found that the oldest member was eighty-four and the youngest eighteen, we would say the membership age range was sixty-six years (eighty-four minus eighteen).

In studying data, one is always interested in knowing how meaningful or typical an average is. The *standard deviation* is valuable in comparing groups. Table 11 shows the wages of the four men and four women who work for Jean's Book Store. The mean of each group is $7,500. For which group, however, is the mean the most descriptive measure? The men's wages are grouped from $6,000 to $9,000, with two above and two below the mean. The women, however, have only one (Jean, who makes $20,000) above the mean and three who are well below it. With the standard deviation we can get an idea of the relevance of the mean to the whole group.

TABLE 11 / Wages in Jean's Book Store

Men	*Women*
$9,000	$20,000
8,000	4,000
7,000	3,000
6,000	3,000
$30,000	$30,000
$\bar{X} = \$7,500$	$\$\bar{X} = \$7,500$

The formula for computing the standard deviation is

$$S \text{ or } \sigma = \sqrt{\Sigma \frac{(X - X)^2}{N}}$$

Where

S or σ = standard deviation
X = the value of any observation
$\overline{X}$ = the mean of all observations
N = the total number of observations

Table 12 calculates the standard deviation (σ) from the data in table 11. As you can see, for men it is $1,118, which is not too large for a $\overline{X}$ of $7,500. For women, however, it is $7,228, almost as large as $\overline{X}$ itself.

Distribution

In data gathering, we often accumulate large masses of numbers. The numbers have little meaning until they are broken down into groups and arranged in some kind of numerical order. A *frequency distribution* is an arrangement of numerical data to indicate the frequency of occurrence of the different values of the variables. Sometimes it will be more meaningful to group scores into categories. If data are to be grouped, it is best that the number of groups does not exceed fifteen and that all groups should have the same internal interval except for the top and bottom groups, which may be left open to accommodate extreme scores.

Table 13 shows the wages of all eight people who work at Jean's Book Store grouped into a frequency distribution. Making a frequency distribution is an exercise in judgment and care. Section A of table 13 is fairly good, but since the wages are all in whole number $1,000 amounts, the wages tend to be near the edge of a category, not distributed evenly within it. In section B there are too many small categories; this is no better than the whole array itself. In section C these defects are corrected. Note, of course, that all three sections do not overlap (what would you do with a $5,000 item if you had $4,000-$5,000 and $5,000-$6,000 groups?), and they are all of the same interval ($1,000 intervals in section B and $2,000 in

TABLE 12 / Standard Deviation of Wages in Jean's Book Store,
Calculated from Data in Table 11

MEN

Item	$\bar{X}-X$	$(\bar{X}-X)^2$
$9,000	7,500 − 9,000 = −1,500	2,250,000
8,000	7,500 − 8,000 = −500	250,000
7,000	7,500 − 7,000 = 500	250,000
6,000	7,500 − 6,000 = 1,500	2,250,000
		5,000,000 = $\Sigma(\bar{X}-X^2)$

$$\sigma = \sqrt{\frac{5,000,000}{4}} = \sqrt{1,250,000} = \$1,118$$

WOMEN

Item	$\bar{X}-X$	$(\bar{X}-X)^2$
$20,000	7,500 − 20,000 = −12,500	156,250,000
4,000	7,500 − 4,000 = 3,500	12,250,000
3,000	7,500 − 3,000 = 4,500	20,250,000
3,000	7,500 − 3,000 = 4,500	20,250,000
		209,000,000 = $\Sigma(\bar{X}-X^2)$

$$\sigma = \sqrt{\frac{209,000,000}{4}} = \sqrt{52,250,000} = \$7,228$$

sections A and C). Also, not one of the sections has gaps where
an amount is left out (note the $4,501 to $5,500 category,
which is included and shown as zero in section B).

Occasionally, we wish to describe a given group in terms of
the total number of cases that have appeared up to and
including that bracket. When we use *cumulative frequencies,* we
are saying that in our distribution each interval includes not
only its own frequency but also the sum of all the frequencies
below it.

TABLE 13 / Frequency Distributions of Wages in Jean's Book Store

[A]

Wage Group	Number in Group
$3,000 – $5,000	3
5,001 – 7,000	1
7,001 – 9,000	3
9,001 and over	1
	8

[B]

Wage Bracket	Number in Group
Under $3,500	2
3,500 – 4,500	1
4,501 – 5,500	0
5,501 – 6,500	1
6,501 – 7,500	1
7,501 – 8,500	1
8,501 – 9,500	1
9,501 and over	1
	8

[C]

Wage Groups	Number in Group
Under $3,500	2
3,501 – 5,500	1
5,501 – 7,500	2
7,501 – 9,500	1
9,500 and over	2
	8

Source: Table 11

Measurements of many kinds of behavior tend to be distributed symmetrically and to bunch around the mean. Much investigation has shown that there is a typical behavior distribution that can be expressed mathematically. This distribution when graphed forms a bell shape. The mean divides the distribution into halves, each of which contains 50 percent of the measures. In a *normal distribution* the mean and the median would be the same. As we have seen earlier, a more common case occurs where high values cause the mean to be higher than the median. The area between the mean and the point one standard deviation *above* the mean includes approximately one-third of the measures: 34.13 percent. Since we have noted that our *normal curve* is symmetrical, the same amount of area is represented on the other side between the mean and the point one deviation *below* the mean. This is the basis for the common notation that 68.26 percent of the items will always be found between +1 SD and −1 SD in a normal curve. Figure 1 illustrates a normal curve.

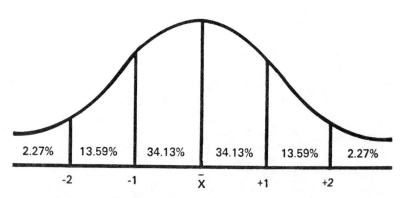

Fig. 1. Areas under the Normal Curve

Standard Scores

Scores are meaningful only in terms of how they compare to other scores. If two different examinations are given, it may be difficult to compare the two scores. One way to make scores more meaningful is by expressing them in terms of *percentile rank,* a rank order score based on a scale of 100. When a score is converted to a percentile rank, the number tells what percentage of individuals had scores lower than the one cited. The 50th percentile is the same as the median. The 99th percentile is the highest score usually cited.

A useful transformation involves *standard scores* or *Z scores,* which yield a score distribution with a mean of zero and a standard deviation of one. A *deviation score* which is attained by subtracting the mean from each original score expresses the distance of an original score from the mean. A standard score expresses that distance in terms of standard deviation. *T scores* are standard scores converted so that all score values are positive with a mean of 50 and standard deviation of 10.

CORRELATION AND REGRESSION

A considerable portion of scientific research in the social sciences is concerned with the relationship between variables. The term *correlation* refers to the degree of relationship between two variables. Correlation suggests two factors increasing or decreasing together. For example, college-educated people have a high rate of voting turnout. Grade-school-educated people are less likely to vote. We would say that there is a *positive correlation* between education and voting. A correlation can also be *negative* with one item increasing as another decreases. For example, the unemployment rate of people with only a grade-school education is higher than that of people with a college education. As education goes up, unemployment goes down.

A *correlation coefficient* is an index of relationship between variables. When two variables are positively correlated so that a high score on one is associated with a high score on the other, the coefficient will be 1.0, the highest possible value a coefficient can have. A perfect negative coefficient of correlation will be −1.0. When there is no relationship between the two variables, the correlation coefficient will be zero. The most commonly used measure of correlation is the *Pearson product-moment correlation coefficient,* symbolized by *r.* The student should become acquainted with this frequently used statistical technique. Another useful correlation coefficient is the *Spearman rank correlation coefficient.* It correlates ranks rather than amounts.

Relationships between two variables can be plotted on a graph, which is often called a *scattergram.* A straight line can then be plotted that relates specific values of one variable to values of the other. In the graph (figure 2) used to illustrate correlations, the scores of one of the variables are represented on the abscissa (horizontal line), the scores of the second variable on the ordinate (vertical line). For example, the X value on the horizontal axis could be age, the Y value on the vertical axis could be income. (The item regarded as the causal or *independent* variable is X.) When two variables are highly correlated, the plotted points tend to be very close to the straight line. This line is called a *line of regression*, and the equation of this line of regression is called a *regression equation.*

The data shown in table 14 will be used to demonstrate these points. If we study incomes, we might try to see if there is a correlation between income and education and between income and age. Table 14 shows for five hypothetical people the age, income, and education of each. In figure 2 a dot is plotted for each person at the point indicated for education and income. The same thing is done with age and income in figure 3. In such a case as figure 2, the coefficient of correlation would

TABLE 14 / Incomes, Ages, and Education

	Income	Age	Education
A	$8,000	32	16 years
B	4,000	22	10 years
C	12,000	40	19 years
D	6,000	50	12 years
E	7,000	35	14 years

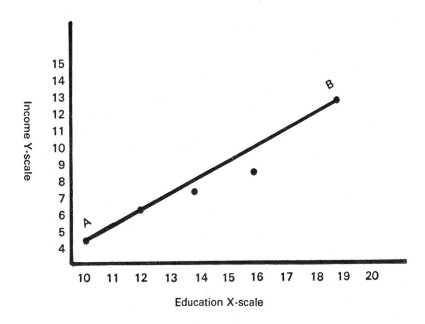

Fig. 2. Graph of Correlation of Income and Education

be .9 or more. Figure 3 shows the case where there is a positive correlation, but it is not as close as in figure 2. The points on the scattergram are not as close to the line. Perhaps *r* would be about .4 here. Age is positively correlated to income. Education, however, is much more highly correlated to income.

A principal aim of all research is prediction. When two variables are correlated, regression equations can be used to predict what value of variable Y would be most likely to be associated with a given value of X. It is also possible to have *multiple correlations* where we could study simultaneously the influence of both age and education on income.

INFERENTIAL STATISTICS

As was mentioned previously, the purpose of *inferential* statistics is to assist in making inferences and judgments about what exists on the basis of only partial evidence. The data used

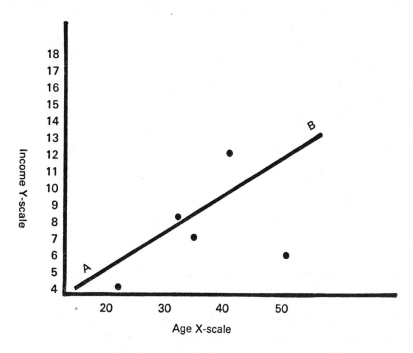

Fig. 3. Graph of Correlation of Income and Age

will most often be drawn from a random sample from which one hopes to be able to draw conclusions about populations. The possibility always exists that the results obtained in the study do not denote a true relationship between variables but instead are the results of sampling error. Two possible errors exist. A *type I* error is committed when a hypothesis is rejected but is true, and a *type II* error exists when the hypothesis is retained but is false. Statistical tests have been developed to make it less likely that the researcher will make these errors.

Significance levels commonly used are .05 and .01. The .05 level means that there is less than a 5 percent probability that the result occurred by chance; .01 means that there is less than 1 percent probability that the results occurred by chance. There are many different kinds of tests, and each one is appropriate only under certain circumstances. The *T-test* is used with a small sample of thirty or less. The T-test stems from the

T-distribution, which is merely an adjustment of the normal distribution we have discussed.

Chi square is a statistical test that can be used to compare two frequency distributions or two cross tabulations in order to determine if there is a significant difference between them. It is usually used to compare a set of observed frequencies with a set of hypothetical frequencies. In order to interpret the numerical value obtained for chi square and thus see whether or not the difference is significant, it is necessary to use a special *chi square table,* which is usually found in the back of statistical textbooks.

Table 15 shows an application of chi square. A researcher goes into a neighborhood and asks twenty men and twenty women their political party preference. Of the forty people, thirty (or 75 percent) are Democrats. The breakdown by sex is shown in table 15. It is observed that eighteen of the twenty men are Democrats and only twelve of the twenty women. If the 75 percent preference of the overall group applied to each sex, we would have expected fifteen men and fifteen women to be Democrats. Is the difference in political preference between men and women real or just due to chance? The chi square test can help us decide. As shown in table 15, the chi square is 4.8. For a two-row by two-column table a .05 chi square must be over 3.84 and a .01 must be over 6.64. Since 4.8 is over 3.84 but not over 6.64, we can conclude that there is only between a 1 percent and a 5 percent probability that our results are due only to chance or sampling error.

STATISTICAL TRAPS TO WATCH FOR

Trust and Distrust of Statistics

To make inferences or positive statements based on statistics requires great care. Students tend to pass through two stages in their attitudes toward statistical conclusions. At first, they tend to accept them and the interpretations placed on them uncritically. Then, they come to distrust statistics entirely

TABLE 15 / Sample Chi Square

		20 Men	*20 Women*
10 Republicans		O = 2 E = 5	O = 8 E = 5
30 Democrats		O = 18 E = 15	O = 12 E = 15

O	E	O−E	(O−E)²	$\frac{(O-E)^2}{E}$
2	5	−3	9	1.8
18	15	3	9	.6
8	5	3	9	1.8
12	15	−3	9	.6
				4.8

$$X^2 = \Sigma \frac{(O-E)^2}{E}$$

Where

X^2 = chi square
E = expected frequencies
O = observed frequencies
R = number of rows
C = number of columns
df = (R−1)(C−1) = (2−1)(2−1) = 1×1 = 1*

. . . .

*In order to adjust for possible cells in table, a measure called degrees of freedom must be calculated. This is done by multiplying the number of rows minus one by the number of columns minus one.

and assert that statistics can prove anything. It is very easy consciously or unconsciously to draw inferences and conclusions from statistical data that are not proved by the data and are in fact erroneous. Statistical data are often only approximations or proxies to the real information sought by the researcher.

Interpretations of numerical or statistical data depend on good logic or what is sometimes called "ordinary clear thinking." It is the logic of mathematics that is so helpful in the analysis of quantitative data. However, mathematics improperly used can confuse the reader and enable one to make false analysis of data seem convincing.

Common Misuses and Abuses of Statistics

One of the oldest jokes among statisticians, often attributed to the humorist Mark Twain, is that "figures never lie, but liars always figure." In a world where number is so popular as a means of analysis, comparison, and justification for action, the possible misuse and abuse of statistics has become commonplace. The beginning researcher cannot be expected to detect the more subtle forms of quantitative deception, but the main ones should become familiar. That provides insurance against being misled by duplicitous statistical presentations and also prevents the unwitting abuse and misuse of statistics in one's own research. Following is a compilation of the more common misuses of statistics as they have been accumulated by statisticians, political scientists, and other quantitative social scientists over a period of time.

SHIFTING DEFINITIONS

Definitions must be correct and consistent when one studies quantitative relationships. A case in point is unemployment. It is not possible to go out and count all the unemployed each day. If we could there would be many questionable cases. Is a twelve-year-old boy or girl who has a whim to work after school to be counted as unemployed? If that student happens to have a job, should he or she be counted as employed when calculating percentages? Most would likely say no, but at what age and under what conditions do we say yes? How such questions are answered greatly affects the calculation of the percent unemployed.

From year to year how these questions are answered may change, or conditions may change, so that the "answers" really mean something different. Different countries answer these questions differently, so one must be very careful when comparing unemployment from year to year or from country to country. Thus, changes in definitions, in emphasis, and in classification, must be noted very carefully if comparisons are to be drawn.

The student also needs to read carefully the table descriptions from the data source. For instance, wage rates and wages earned are very different concepts. In fact, one may go up while the other goes down. Using one when it is believed that the other applies would create false interpretations. A study of the descriptions and footnotes of tables will enable one to escape this kind of error.

MISUSES DUE TO INACCURATE MEASUREMENT OF CLASSIFICATION

Crime statistics are illustrative of the problem of inaccurate measurement or classification. Because the exact method of reporting crime has been inconsistent, and related variables such as age makeup of the population are always changing, it is very difficult to measure crime and classify cases accurately and consistently. Thus, crime statistics have limited use in analyzing trends in crime. A serious error in research paper writing is in placing reliance on statistical analysis when the analysis was not correctly performed or when it is being used for some purpose different from that which the person making the analysis expected it to be used.

The more sophisticated and complex the analysis is, the more apt it is to be misused. Statistical pitfalls may include mistakes in recording the data or in performing calculations, since either may produce incorrect information. Also, collecting data that does not measure the phenomenon the student thinks is being measured can produce strikingly erroneous findings. The issue of bias also arises if one gives more weight to facts that support a preconceived opinion than to conflicting data. There is almost an irresistible tendency to let one's desires or previous experiences influence an evaluation of facts. When that occurs, the statistics are used only as a pretense that the decision had a logical basis.

THE QUESTION OF NONCOMPARABLE DATA

Comparisons are an important part of statistical analysis. But it is extremely important that these comparisons be made only between comparable sets of data. Comparison of costs of living at the present time with costs of living fifty years ago raises questions of comparability. Many of the items in the present-day budget either did not exist or were relatively unimportant fifty years ago. In comparing from one period to another the number of deaths attributed to a particular disease, the more recent year may show an increased rate due to a more accurate reporting of the causes of death. Hence, the figures for the two periods would not be strictly comparable.

UNCRITICAL PROJECTION OF TRENDS

Erroneous projection of trends has done much to discredit the use of statistical analysis. It is often not helpful to simply project past trends into the future. It is true that the only basis on which to forecast the future is the record of the past, but one must examine very carefully and search for all the possibilities why a past trend may not continue into the future. Before one can simply project the future on the basis of the growth in the past years, it is necessary to make a careful analysis to determine the factors that might have caused that growth, to see if the factors will be as important in the future and if there are additional factors, both positive and negative, that will be important in future growth.

IMPROPER ASSUMPTIONS REGARDING CAUSATION

It is much easier to measure the relationship between two sets of events than to explain the causes and effects of relationships. One can have an accurate compilation of statistical data that indicates that events happened together, but it is very difficult to determine why they happened together. Often a person may conclude that, because two events have occurred together, one was the cause of the other. Very often a case can be made for either factor being the cause, when actually both events were the result of some third factor. When a judgment must be made in forecasting or concerning other relationships from a cause-and-effect basis, there must be a clear understanding of the phenomena.

CASE SELECTIONS

Another concern in statistical studies is the method of selecting cases. An example of this is mental disease in men and women. If we compare the percent of the male population in mental hospitals with the percent of the female population in mental hospitals and find that the percentage is higher for the male population, this may mean that the incidence of mental disease is higher among men or it may mean that men are more likely to be detected and institutionalized than women. Inappropriate comparisons are closely related to the above. If there are shifting definitions due to shifting composition or correlation, it is often the result of assuming that correlation indicates causation. The real world is filled with many examples of this.

8

Journals of Interest
in Political Science Research

There are two ways that journals can be useful in political science research. First, students may read specific articles in a topic area. The bridges to these articles are the indexes (p. 105) and the digests and abstracts (p. 74) described earlier.

Second, students may browse for ideas. By looking through the relevant journals they can locate current research and ideas that might never reach book form, or if they do, it may be years before they are published. There are literally hundreds of possible journals in which students can browse.

Recently, two political scientists polled their colleagues on the sixty-three journals which they considered most familiar and of highest quality (Michael W. Giles and Gerald C. Wright, Jr., "Political Scientists' Evaluations of Sixty-three Journals," *P.S.* 8, Summer 1975).

We have selected what we believe are the most useful of these journals to the beginning researcher.

GENERAL ACADEMIC JOURNALS

These journals tend to emphasize refined research methodology and articles on highly specialized topics. They are apt to be more difficult for the beginning student, but if your instructor emphasizes the academic discipline of political science, they can be a key source.

These two journals are the most prestigious and familiar:

American Political Science Review. American Political Science Association. 1906–.

The prestigious quarterly journal of the American Political Science Association includes both highly methodological articles such as "Some Problems in Alfred Schultz's Phenomenological Methodology" and process-oriented articles concerned more closely with political behavior such as "Preconditions of Mayoral Leadership."

World Politics: A Quarterly Journal of International Relations. Center of International Studies. Princeton University, 1948–.

This quarterly is the number one choice for quality in the Giles and Wright poll. It is less methodologically oriented than the *American Political Science Review* with much more emphasis on international affairs, i.e., "The Arms Race Phenomenon" and "The Dynamics of the Chinese Revolution."

There are also a number of other academically oriented journals published by regional political science associations. At one time such journals emphasized articles on their particular region. This is less so today, but occasionally one will focus on regional politics. These journals are as follows:

American Journal of Politics (Formerly: *Midwest Journal of Political Science*). Midwest Political Science Association. 1967–. Quarterly.

Journal of Politics. Southern Political Science Association. 1939–. Quarterly.

Polity. Northeastern Political Science Association. 1968–. Quarterly.

Western Political Quarterly. Western Political Science Association. 1948–. Quarterly.

OTHER GENERAL ACADEMIC JOURNALS

Political Science Quarterly. Academy of Political Science. 1886–.

This quarterly places less emphasis on quantitative methodology and is more historically oriented. It contains articles such as "Roosevelt, Truman, and the Atomic Bomb: A Reinterpretation" and "The Politics of the Allende Overthrow in Chile."

JOURNALS IN SUBFIELDS OR CLOSELY RELATED FIELDS TO POLITICAL SCIENCE

The focus of these journals is usually well illustrated by their titles. We have noted a few representative articles where necessary.

Administrative Science Quarterly. Cornell University. 1956–. Quarterly.

"The Interorganizational Network as Political Economy," "Organizational Development and Change in Organizational Performance."

American Behavioral Scientist. Sage, 1957–. Bimonthly.

This journal contains articles on such topics as "The Coming American Welfare State," "The Politics of Environmental Policy," and "Varieties of Political Conservatism." Its focus is interdisciplinary, but when dealing with political topics most of the articles are by political scientists.

American Academy of Political and Social Science Annals. The American Academy of Political and Social Science. 1891–. Bimonthly.

Each issue focuses on a public problem with a mixture of articles by academicians and practitioners. Topics such as "Student Protest," "Propaganda in International Affairs," and "Political Campaigning" are contained in this journal popularly known as "The Annals."

Comparative Politics. City University of New York. 1968–. Quarterly.

"The Japanese Party System in Transition," "Patterns of Political Violence in Comparative Historical Perspective."

Foreign Affairs: An American Quarterly Review. Council on Foreign Relations. 1922–. Quarterly.

Featured are academically-oriented articles by noted practitioners of foreign policy, such as "Foreign Policy, Public Opinion, and Secrecy" by Nicholas de B. Katzenbach, and "Does War Have A Future?" by Louis Halle.

International Affairs. The Royal Institute of International Affairs. 1922–. Quarterly.

The articles, such as "International Terrorism: Problems of Definition" and "The Future of Industrialism," show a non-quantitative British-oriented view of foreign relations.

Journal of Conflict Resolution (Formerly: *Conflict Resolution*). Sage, 1957–. Quarterly.

The focus of the research is on war and peace between and within nations. While emphasizing conflict resolution, many of the articles are highly methodological, such as "Measuring Systematic Polarity," "On the Economic Theory of Alliances."

Political Theory: An International Journal of Political Philosophy. Sage, 1973–. Quarterly.

The title implies the contents, such as " 'Facts' and 'Values' in Politics: Are They Separable?" and "Idealism and Peoples War: Sartre on Algeria."

The Public Interest. National Affairs. 1965–. Quarterly.

The journal contains as broad a view as the title implies. "Toward a Reform of Social Security," "The Pursuit of Health," and "Should Every Job Support a Family?" are examples of articles.

Law and Society Review. Law and Society Association. 1967–. Quarterly.

Emphasized is the relationship between society and the legal process, for example, "Why the 'Haves' Come Out Ahead: Speculations on the Limits of Legal Change."

Political Affairs: Theoretical Journal of the Communist Party. Affairs, 1922–. Monthly.

Although not in the Giles and Wright article, this journal is still the recognized academic journal of Marxist thought and analysis. It contains such articles as "The Struggle for Detente," and "The Energy Rip-Off."

Politics and Society. Department of Political Science. Columbia University, 1970–. Quarterly.

Contributors include political scientists, sociologists, and historians. Examples of articles are "Politics and Unnatural Practice: Political Science Looks at Female Participation," and "The 'Crowd' in the Russian Revolution: Toward Reassessing the Nature of Revolutionary Leadership."

Public Administration Review. American Society of Public Administration. 1940–. Bimonthly.

Frequently issues are devoted to an entire topic such as unionism and public employment or the American city manager. A typical article is "Changing Styles of Planning, Presidential Policy Process, and 'New Administration': A Search for Revised Paradigms."

Public Choice. Center in Public Choice. Virginia Polytechnic Institute, 1966–. Quarterly.

Articles apply a combination of economic and political theory to problems of public choice and decision making. Sample articles are "Some Simple Economics of Voting and Not Voting" and "The Carrot and the Stick: Optimal Program Mixes for Entrepreneural Political Leaders."

Public Opinion Quarterly. Columbia University. 1937–. Quarterly.
"Change in Voting Turnout 1952-1972" and "Are There Bellwether Election Districts?" are sample articles.

Public Policy. John F. Kennedy School of Government. Harvard University, 1970–. Quarterly.
The analysis of public policy issues is nontechnical, for example, "The Design of Property Rights for Air Pollution Control" and "Restructuring the Military Industrial Complex."

Publius: The Journal of Federalism. The Center for the Study of Federalism. Temple University, 1971–. Quarterly.
The articles show a broad interdisciplinary view of the relations of nonsovereign political entities. Sample articles are "Federal Provincial Conflict in Canada" and "State Boundaries and Political Cultures: An Exploration in the Tri-State Area of Michigan, Indiana, and Ohio."

Urban Affairs Quarterly. Sage, 1965–. Quarterly.
Sample articles are "Education Incentive Plans for the Police" and "Electing Blacks to Municipal Office."

JOURNALS IN OTHER DISCIPLINES RELATED TO POLITICAL SCIENCE

The following journals all include some politically relevant articles from the perspective of another discipline.

Sociology is the other social science discipline most closely related to contemporary political science. Almost all behavior we identify as "political" can be at least partially explained in terms of some sociological concept such as class, race, or bureaucratization. Note the examples in the following journals.

American Journal of Sociology. University of Chicago Press, 1895–. Bimonthly.

Articles are heavily methodological, such as "The Impact of City on Racial Attitudes," and "Organizational Inequality: The Case of the Public Employment Agencies."

American Sociological Review. American Sociological Association. 1936–. Bimonthly.

Sample articles are "Aging, Voting and Political Interest," "Power Opinion and Social Circles: A New Methodology for Studying Opinion Makers."

Social Forces. The Southern Sociological Society. 1922–. Quarterly.

Sample articles are "White Attitudes Toward Black People" and "Class Consciousness and American Political Attitudes."

Social Science Quarterly (Formerly: *Southwestern Social Science Quarterly*). Southwestern Social Science Association. 1920–. Quarterly.

Sample articles are "Oppression and Power: The Unique Status of the Black Woman in the American Political System" and "Participation in Local Policy Making: The Care of Referenda."

Daedelus. American Academy of Arts and Sciences. 1958–. Quarterly.

The focus is on broad interdisciplinary issues with particular emphasis on the humanities. Usually one issue is devoted to a particular topic such as "Historical Studies Today," "The Future Metropolis," and "Students in Revolt."

Index

T

2 3 4 5 6 7 8 9 10—B—84 83 82 81 80 79 78 77 76